Raw Dreamers

What's been your catastrophic event?

Arsalan Akhter

PARTRIDGE

A Penguin Random House Company

To order additional copies of this book, contact
Partridge India
000 800 10062 62
www.partridgepublishing.com/india
orders.india@partridgepublishing.com

To the nature of God
To the parents
To the beautiful people of my country: Nepal

Author's Note

I choose this book to be unedited by any professional, no grammatical quotient getting corrected for the sake to present the readers what a fifteen year old can replicate the translations to a 26 year old man. This remains raw for the sake of writing ego.
Belief!!

Dedicated to all the people who believed that failing was just as important as it is to succeed today.

PROLOGUE

---

*V*ery much like every other young boy, Amen too is fussed up into the magnificent sounding words—"Cherish your dream, live your life"
He is strangled into a big mind when he is fifteen years old and decides that he is meant to be in the Indian Cricket team but his sky-scraping mind suddenly goes to burial ground when he receives the news of having failed in the 9th grade.

He holds his fantasies tight, thereon. The idea of leaving home is just delayed and not rejected.

Amen's mom makes him understand the actual achievement from life, it stands out as the novel's justifiable philosophy with which the actual journey of the boy starts. This story is narrated by a twenty-six year "half old, half young man" who gets camouflaged secret delivered by God.

Entwined in the family issues, the boy struggles but does not at any point of time stoops to all these demands. Despite being involved from neck to toe, he fights to keep his dreams untouched, unblemished and undented, and such was his resolve. He longs to disappear, to fly away to larger horizons and make a man of himself. He feels like a nestling; waiting for the sunny day when he would soar the skies. So he keeps fluttering his wings at his nest, looks and sighs at the limitless sky. He wished to foresee what future had in store for him and he just couldn't wait . . . . Familiar string, friend's closeness, father's debt, sister's talk—nothing restrains his dream as to get mere forgetful. He disappears from the sights of family for exactly one year, and announces of his well-being only through e-mails, which emotionalizes the whole journey abstractly. The more he goes ahead, the more people he meets, the girl he finds perfect, the camouflage secret he gets, everything screeches down to his achievement.

Achievement with a new definition.

Thousands dream can't match up for what Amen achieves

Acknowledgements:

*T*hank God!
Today, I am in a position to draft the acknowledgement page.

The list has to be long as many people lay behind the architects of this book.

It was the 45 minute drive in the bus from school to home when I would sit at the back seat structuring beautiful sounding poems where all of this writing habit took its first plunge of flight.

It was Rupa for whom I would craft letters at DPS and exchanged and she would everytime appall me of my good English writing.
It was Garima Lohani and companion with whom I had my teenage moments at tuition classes.
It was Abhishek and Ashitosh having companied me at a very difficult phase of time.

It was Azhmat (Sonu) funnily being my best friend and the only one to have made it to the adulthood friendlist from childhood.

It was Azhan bhai for having scripted the response so positive in the early phase of this novel.

It was Ram, Nikhil, Harish, Jay, Ashutosh and Ankit to have an awesome time everyday in the bus.

I must thank Hitesh dai for sharing his delicious tiffin when we most needed at the end of each hectic day and Aditya bhai who was the successor later.

Thanks to Ayan, Mandip, Khushbu, Prity, Asmika, Sapana, RIP, Susman, Ankit for being good.
Thanks Manisha, Pallavi, Kanika Arora and the whole army from science batch.
Thanks to Asmita for being a kind counterpart in the sports captain tenure, without any tussles.

Thanks Arun sir, Neeraj sir, RuchiMa'm, Monica Ma'm, Gobardan sir and other teaching fraternities from DPS.
Thank you principal Ma'am—Neelam Pal, your morning assembly words has always inspired me (though at some days, it was only about announcing the fee defaulter's list, except those!)

Thanks needs to be shared with the 'soom' group who were the fuel for surviving in my one year lived time at Kathmandu—Dibin, Bibek, Ishan, Nirmal, Wangla, Shishir, Karpur and Sunir.

Double thanks to Sunir and Karpur for having the morning bike ride to college. It was great help man!

Thanks to many other kcmiites for being kind. It was great to lose that cricket match. Paras dai, you still remain the culprit for the last bowl you bowled.

Thanks Deepesh for believing in my over ambitious project and santosh dai for your support.

IshworiMa'm, Thanks!!

Thanks to Vaibhav, Mohit, Ojesh, Pratik, Shreyansh. I hope you guys remember our commitment to play cricket matches at class 5.

Sunil, Those pipes were real hard!!

Thanks to Mallika for introducing me to this name.

Thanks to Ankit for believing in my young ideas.

Thanks to the other Ankit also with whom days has been ever so enriching though things are different now.

Thanks Deepika for criticizing me a lot.

Thanks to Manoj Jaishi.

Thanks to Yuga Shrestha for many reasons.

Thanks to Aamir bhai.

And at the end, I must thank two most important people again and again—First, "my dad" for being the most correct inspiration to my life whose struggles has been

phenomenal and it's been a treat to be in it from so very before.
And this creature in anybody's life is awesome—"mom"

Thanks to God!!

Chapter-1

K hudi ko kar buland itna ke har taqdeer se pehle
Khuda bande se puche bata teri raza kya hai

When Allama Iqbal wrote these lines, he must have been unimaginable to what could people ask, and how far could have God given to these ever asking piece of specie.

I had not asked for what I have got today. I am at my running age of 26, half old, half young, less intelligent, more emotional.

It was five years back when I had left home to search something, complying the world's fashion—'Find yourself!'

It was six years back when I started my study in pursuit of a bachelor's degree.

It was seven years back when I passed class 12th marking a big achievement.

Today I got the news from GOD.

I wasn't waiting for this news.
But today's morning dripped not only with stupendous light but with the news from God.

Yes God!

The fog now settled in the newly made pebbled road outside my home, whence human eyes could go blinking for hours, but the fog not leaving its commitment.
Making it hard for the human eye to find a vision.

The rooster from somebody's home crowed its natural alarm, dew drops kissed the petals, sun still hiding its presence.
It's a time when all the drunken people last night will wake up perfectly normal. All children in rage with their parents last night will wake up sober. Each individual would ready to compete himself to fight with the world's population.

A new day has kicked off.

What separates fog and smog is color.
From those white vapors emerged a man in white, semi translucent, something of him to tell your senses in one attempt—'Angel'
An angel sent by God to handover the news uncaring of my reaction to take back.
Even if he cared, I had nothing to react.

The sun that arose today had the power to burn me; it hadn't come this bright in my life ever before. Maybe, it was all because of the news.

I knew the almighty always have amazing plans for all of us, but why!
Why is the news always amazing?

In this early winter morning of 26 December, 2011 at the while sitting casually at the portico of my house, I had this amazement.
I had this amazement of listening to the news.
The messenger handed me this news in the shells of a secret: NOT TO BE TOLD TO ANYONE

It itched to me, inability of shouting to the world about the most benevolent news ever heard is a near to death silence.
God had his play with almost all the members of this earth. We are his creation, he has the right to do so but does he not see the caliber in pain.
Why didn't the messenger's flying legs stopped in the air realizing what he was giving me—"A secret"
If I ever have a chance to question God, it would surely be, "why do I get this?"
And, "why today?"

I don't know.
I am a simple man as you, as the one sitting beside you and as the one not sitting beside you. I am alike everyone else.

I am Amen.

I will tell you my life.
I don't know what I will tell and what you will perceive at the end of the story.

Think about a movie, you had seen some years back displaying a flashback.

Everybody's life is melodramatic in the same way or other.

My story starts from where I can remember, ofcourse!!
Little more than ten years down the line—Back to 2000

That was a millennium year, whence all babies born were termed millennium babies, a useless problem as Y2K was being given so much importance, the billionth living person in India was born, concord—the fastest aircraft had crashed in a hotel, our neighboring country—India in the prime ministerial tenure of Mr. Vajpayee had created 3 new states and my own country Nepal was witnessing a new revolutionary leader—'Prachanda' who had arisen as a name seizing terror in the minds of general public. Some even regarded him 'God' for his unseen image doing all the activities.

This year amid all the worldly activities was a tensed one at home.
A feud had cropped in between my father and his brothers—"It was a separation"

"Everything is good when a separation happens as so many changes comes in," concluded my 15 and a half year old mind. The only bad thing dad did on this while was, he left 'everything'—home, factory, cars, everything.
That meant our ravishing life could just turn upside down, into a struggling phase.

The separation papers were ready. Big stamps on the paper, black coat people resurgent on the drawing room, some *mullas* present as well for the Islamic point of view, constant sullen face from dad—all suggesting 'Aqram Iraqi Hosseini is getting separated' that was my father.

Little more days we lived in the same house until dad could find another or make another one. Home-making was no easy job.

Some author had written it, and I heard very clearly from my father, "Discouragement is a deadly disease"

He was sourly discouraged, bitterly anxious and ragingly furious.

My mother had a way of explaining things that we could understand and if she happened to be in the mood, she could turn the tornado like destruction into a heavenly pleasing breath.

We had yet not seen the phase of poverty, the phase of hard-life, the phase of sheer struggle but now it looked nothing was far away.

Though dad had been in it in his early years, mom was yet not into it at any part of her life and maybe so she had those good words always to offer.

She filled us, particularly dad with encouragement, passion for a new inventive beginning from when on people left marking the end.

This was the sole reason why dad had become yet again passionate.

On exactly eighth day of the announcement of separation, uncle said to mom in that dusty afternoon, "Hmm, we need to paint this room as to the room looks energetic again"

That was a signal—"Go fast"

That same evening, when dad came home after his routine search for home, he wasn't any happy either.

He was sad as he had been in each day of the week's evening. The signal was relayed and he at once flustered, "We need to get moving from tomorrow"

I was the one listening everything, witnessing everything.

Two of elder brothers were far in the hostels of Delhi knowing nothing of the proceedings, one sister though two years elder was customized in the tradition of being a girl, a mute watcher in the notion of 'what can I do'

There was nothing I could do as well, I could just transmit the highest level of pain that my parents were suffering and that was it, that was the limit!

Next day onwards, we had to start the transfer.

Dad had bought a good piece of land and the construction had begun but for the time being, we had to live somewhere else.

One of dad's kind friend had asked us to live in their house and we got the upper floor for ourselves.

Nobody was happy.

It was one of those few days, when mom asked me not to go school the next day.

I wasn't happy of not going school this time because I was sad for the reason.

We had little talks in the evening about our actions from now on. Dad was giving little lectures which was okay to hear. We were not to have any 'good' pre-conceived notions of the new place, about how to start the transfer, how to coordinate and how to carry the emotions most importantly.

The next phase of our family was to get started from tomorrow. What I remember of the transfer day is that we were shifting from our house to a dad's friend home that was watchably near to our under-construction area.

I was taking bags of material that was handed to me by my mother in that trans-shifting period . . .

It was a nice feeling because some change was now to occur and also that mom was entrusting me with materialistic handling work.

I asked mom, "What time will it be, that we get shifted?"
She looked at the watch respecting my ask, announced any number that came in her view—2

I was excited with a wow '2'

The best thing in the home we were shifting was that a boy lived there who was same as to my age or 4-5 months elder to me—Rian.

He was to become one of my most intimate buddies.

I went to the home, Rian had already started following me like a tail, we waited for the time to click 2 and as it did, I announced as it was my first feat achieved—"I have shifted now"

Rian was the only one showing teeth, giggling, gasping, clapping in amazement like a child and clasping in wonder with excitement.

'What a child he is' I garnished and smarted within

He also had come on to believe with me that when the clock gongs 2, things would be official: he would be officially shifted, we would be officially friends, officially home-mates, etc, etc.

But there was 'nothing official about it'

His sister, 4 years elder was a sighful watcher, heaving and realizing the burden of added members at home.

Mother or father were yet not to be seen at the vicinity. I was uninterested and unrealized for what sigh was dad giving at the while of leaving home that he had once made by his own hands. What cleavage of disturbance was mom facing to leave the home where she had spent her 23 years of married life.

Anyways I was officially shifted.

I and Rian woke up at 6 on holidays, with my dirty grey track suit put over for the whole day. It was incredible as it never made me come out of the sporty sensation.

Very soon, I was organizing matches with 2 rupees from each of the player and got double on the wins.

Everybody glared a reason for not presenting that sum of rupee.

I had no much reason but only the sake of cricket that I would take away those small sums from my father's pocket when he was asleep.

I loved it!

Because then a match was sure to get played.

On match days, we had to catch up all the players from their houses—Khurram, Tarzan, Tariq, almost all.

Khurram's father would argue very kindly, "he has to go to the shop" in a quenching voice trying to attend accountability of the old age that he had reached, shivering his head and highlighting his walking stick on hand.

He swayed his walking stick in the air while he talked. I sensed its other purpose—it was a threat!

My arguments always remained indifferent that today's match was almost the most important one!

Tarzan, he was really a Tarzan. Never at home, running from here to there, we had to link up his relatives and go 3-4 places as per their 'maybe Tarzan is there'

Then exhausted, lubricated, sweats sprinkling from head to internal parts, we would find him.

As those two old and fabricated doors would open, we would find him cuddling a baby, popping him up on the air, whooing on the ear, so happy as if he was living his life.

Stupid!

On asking ferociously 'what man?'

He would not answer but shrewdly flaunt his hands on the thin line of growing moustache, looking miserable with the small face that his shoulder beheld. It was a learned and practiced trick of Tarzan to diverge our mind towards the opponents "they are too tough this time" with an eloquence of craftiness.

Khurram would suddenly grow energetic with fury at this point, "Are we less?"

This way Tarzan never answered of being lost on the match days, shifting our momentum to the passionate part. We realized this feature of him only the next time we would be after his call.

We three still had enough to call. I said watching my only clock that in the group comprised of, "45minutes more to the match."
Khurram bent himself, not disturbing me, trying to adjust the exactness, "it's 47 minutes" in an ingenuity pride.

Rian, my home mate would still be in the toilets or sleeping or drinking tea with bread enveloped on it. He never came with us on the first call, made himself count valuable. After lot of urging and upon understanding that the request and buttering from us could get exhausted any now and then.
Just on next moment, it was quite vulnerable that we would not give a damn whether he comes with us or not; he would ask for five extra minutes pleading, as if he was still in the mode of a football match and additional time was the rule of the game.
We moved further with the calling and upon reaching Tariq's house, he would be readying and thudding his pad and gloves, they all together proceeded to the field.

I would run to Yassar and Rafey's house, they first of all handed me the 2 rupee note reacting as they are now totally legible and to ask for batting up in the order was a part of their birth right. I requested them to take their MRF unplayable bat so that the opponents take us seriously.
The players all the time got shortened and so I always had a backup with Zeeshan as the last call, he had a benefit

along with him, he had a brother-Babu; so in last urgency we would often take him as well.

I would reach the field but Rian would not have arrived yet. The match time would have almost clicked.
The idiot opponents still would be far off sight, always late. Just then we found two members of the opponents knocking bats on the other end of the ground.
Tariq would generously go and invite them to knock with us while their team is still unarrived.

Just as he tucked one shot out of ten, Khurram would reach up to the batsman in a leisurely manner and flatter, "Hmm you seem to be the best batsman in your team."
That fellow with kindness on showy part but actually fear on the inside part of heart to the already calculated risk of 8 on 2 inside his mind, swiftly pronounced the names of their best batsmen.
Such way, we would know about the opponents and all of the team members with their analysis, reacted as gold was on our pocket.

Yassar, exactly at this point articulated to Rafey, "This is the reason we come early in the field then the opponents" displaying his 3 months seniority with a piece of advice.
Now the opponents would arrive, handy in equipment, beaming with confidence, rendering with capabilities and smearing with surety. Rafey ready with his fingers to point 'that Kapil is the fastest bowler' and all ran their eyes in astonishment: who . . . who?

Matches we won; matches we lost!
Let's say matches we lost; and sometimes we won!

But all matches had a stake of reputation, all of us had an individual say at respective places for what happened about the match and often saying 'we lost' tended us to get peculiar in reactions.

Often Yassar's sister would advise him not to play any other match again or Khurram's father would complain, "this was the consequence of leaving shop on a match day." So, if involvement of everybody meant cricket as a religion then I knew it was a growing religion in our *mohalla*.

During our ongoing matches, when all namazis from the mosque which was at a good seeable distance hovered around the ground, watched our play as fine spectators and gave their united reactions on taking a wicket or on even bowling a dot ball on important occasions. I sensed what religious cricket meant at that age in this corner of Nepal.

Most of all, the senior team of *mohalla* would always be eyeing on our performances and the best one always had a chance to be in the senior team, and being in the senior team meant that even the walking stride announced of a pride among the juniors.

This match we had won by some techniques. We brought in the senior teammate—Amjad into our team as he looked one of us and he tucked out well in the middle.

Rian was a character that I sought to have true expressions from but if he was happy he would show as if 'this was nothing' and if he was sad he would show something different.

We fully utilized sun's light with all kind of activities but the light would end up at around 6, and with that morning's tracksuit I and Rian would reach home feeling proud of what we did all day.

My mother had the same staunching words that she gave every Saturday; father would have his reputation reserved for important occasions.

After Saturday, it was Sunday-a working day or to say it with more concerned view—a schooling day.

The morning always had the same look—'You're getting late, buddy!'

It was a complete displeasure to come out of the rejuvenating Saturday and line up with next 6 days of tight schooling schedule.

I hated that scent of books which I opened at around seven in the evening after the *kunchi* maulana was gone giving the Arabic and Urdu teachings. I never opened my book to study but only to show that I was studying.

I had known in around class 5th that there was no use of me studying when my brother claimed that he made me pass and I was 'dragged' further when I was still recovering from the appendices operation. I didn't know the authenticity of his claim but I had been tonged up onto strong realization that I wasn't meant for this stuff.

The school was such a dreadful place, my heart would shrink whenever I got into the premises, maths sir had his own world of geometry to convey which I still think is in some way of delivering process. The language teacher had her own complicated process to make us rot all the meanings of the world that could barely come into use at any part of time. Science, I thought was some logic if I ever could catch up but the understandings department of my mind was unacceptable for it and had lost the rope so the delivery department of science all the time complained "I didn't get the rope so I didn't get in your mind"

Among all I think English was most understandable because I loved reading poems and stories of any kind from little age but it was a different matter that I never got to show my love in the scoresheets.

I had a simple thought; what's that school giving me where I am all confused!

My sister Faiza was something . . . something for me

She was two classes senior to me and often we would go home together and it was on her recommendation that I had got into the useless morning tuition to a pathetically beautiful teacher. I really had any kind of efforts ready for her; I mean Faiza.

When we would leave school, I patronized infront of Faiza displaying 'my gang'

I waited for her outside or she waited if her assembled house came outside first. Then we would buy a foodstuff called *chaku* (food stuff) costing just a rupee but was an expense very dear to me. So I would try and pursue Faiza most of the time to pay money from her bag where she always had around 20 rupees but became dear to her as soon as I asked, otherwise she would have mindlessly spend them with Harpiiiiiinder and pravaaaaaa; her friends.

Those were the times when I almost realized that we were into real financial crisis and so at first I stopped rickshaw a little before reaching home so that he took 8 rupees instead of 10 and then I started walking school and came back the same way.

That was the time, when my father had just separated and had an entity to make again. For the time being we were residing at a father's friend house which I think is an owe for the rest of my life.

I realized the crunch of financial crisis when my mom knowing I had walked all the way would not ask me to hire a rickshaw again and upon returning that 20 rupees back to mom, her face glowed like a steam on a river and I had no more better moment than that for my entire lived life.

She would be tangled in that happiness of returned money and walked son.

I had lesser emotions for Faiza than my mom. I saw mom one day bringing bucket of water up to the three floors and on some other day crutched in fever and father applying his own medicinal techniques to save that 200 rupee of doctor's fee. I have written something in rhyme for mom which I would like to read out on some special occasion.

I WANNA BACK THE TIME

I was three,
Only I could do was to watch a tree.
I had to go for the classes,
classes for the very first time.
I wore a shoe,
a pant . . . all in blue.

I cried a lot,
Even mom had to give a thought
Did I do that?

I then grew a little older,
Mind had senseless demands to make
Mom sorted a reason even more bigger
to dodge me into a fake.

I was eight,
At the gate, I tried to cry for long
What if might mom feel bad to the extent of some
That, now her child is not in need of mom.

A little more bigger
I ran to school . . . without my breakfast.
After breakfast,
Mom would accompany upto the school.
With mom! Would it be cool?

Once again I sobbed,
I was fourteen . . . then I thought
Wasn't I in the years to be at the top!

Then I just had a year for the college
College had an impact of impressions on my mind.

I was twenty
The view said
There was no such thing that I could not do.

I had to go for the classes
classes for the very last time.
I wore a shoe,
A pant all matched with the shoe in blue.

We cried a lot,
Even friends had to give a thought
Did we do that?

Now it was my graduation day
The day I have ever chanted to be in rejoice.

I ran to the port . . . without my breakfast
After breakfast,
Mom and I would be late rather being fast.
Had mom gone back,
Without mom would it be cool?

My mom was back with me
brought together . . . some shiny priceless tears.

I shall take my future in terms of degree
I dare not make it bad.
Worth of my mom's offering that she had
I never had a sincere feeling attached to that.

For that mom! At once
I got all my feelings gathered
Gatherings scattered at once upto the childhood.
Childhood . . . where I have never ever
wanted to be being a child.
But now I wanna back the time.

When I will read this to her, we will cry, cry exactly in the
melodramatic fashion as filmy actors do. And, I will enjoy
every bit of that scene.

Right now, I was too small to understand or stretch a
helping hand to my parents just than to cut something off
from my own expenses. I had stopped taking money from
my father's pocket for the sake of cricket. I had stopped on
chakus, walked all the way. That doubling of 2 rupee from
match victories brought in the thought of helping mom
with that sum but it meant nothing to the comparisons.

My father once came in home, helmet on his left hand,
scrubbing his right hand elbow with two fingers that
was unused with helmet carriage. He announced plainly
as if he had evenly escaped a mild rain, "today I had an
accident!"
When matter went in detail, it was known that he had
directly come in to home not caring of the hospital
because he cared for the bills.
That was growing into a hard process of time. I was
getting mature at that small age; though father never made
me come into a plumped thought that I had to sacrifice
something from me.

I still had my matches going, after the previous victory Yassar's sister had yet not suggested him not to play the next match.

That not coming of complaints were satisfying, but we knew one loss could energize their discouraging spirit anytime.

Every evening when I was back from school, we would all get collected in the field for the play. The site would be something like swami and friends' Malgudi days and I was never more proud when the thought knocked on my mind.

If God had promised to give everything that we wanted in heavens, I would demand him exactly this frame of time.

At this moment, all the boys had only one vow "play" and all the parents had almost a same vow as well "study" which was never paid heed.

My company of friends had changed all this time alongwith father's separation.

Before, Mohit, Ojesh, Vaibhav and many more friends used to come to my home with their parents or sometimes only with a caretaker or a driver and we all played for the whole day in my playing room with sophisticated toys and perhaps all those indoor games. When we drove those remote cars and wheeled planes, we carefully named them as Toyota, Ferrari and other topnotches. It was a lavished form of life.

But, now dad had separated, and separated quite publicly, as an elder brother with generosity.

"But who cares, for who comes from my friend's fraternity, they won't die not coming at me, let their lavishness be with them"—I had settled my mind with this statement.

The place had changed, playing room was far-gone, toys were limited, rooms were few, no Toyota car.

I had to change and I had changed.

I was in a *mohalla* and not in a society. Companions were betterly Tarzan and Khurram. It was obvious to think and have fantasies of doing things at their level of standard. So, the realization came to me that I had never stepped inside a moving bus.

"Okay, we will do that," said Tarzan with an attempt to be serious but cried with laughter adoring at my wish.

I had this passion to make myself know how the stomach churned and gave a giggling effect on continuous driving; how the sleeky vibration in the tyres made us asleep so well, the trees passing and pacing every constant second, how the passage of another big vehicle created a big whhhooaaaa sound turning the set hair on the other side. With these feelings to get, I also had to know whether I would vomit when the bus goes into the heights, Will I be a passenger carrying a polybag all my life?

I got into the bus to cover a distance of around 48 kilometres with Khurram, Rian, Tarzan, Yassar, Tariq, all my best buddies.

Yes, I was now allowed to move alone to a couple of places because my father now wasn't in a situation to provide me with a Toyota car everywhere with the security of driver.

The bus had its own striking features, far different from the car we had. Multitude faces; black, green, white, all kind of people jumbled up on their fairy seats, unknown languages from all those different colored skin people. Nobody belonged to any religion inside, acquiring and crouching seats became the only devotion inside. The bus stopped at a place and all stooped out of the vehicle, different heads acquiring different bushes sprouting the bush from their own sources.

The bus had its genuine reasons to stop time and again. A kid got to go the toilets then somebody got to puke out and this way the drive continues, the journey continues . . .

Here at the mills ground, things never changed.

Some activities always meant to buzz this place. We were never tired to play cricket, sometimes we just got exhausted with the same course of play so we changed to football, sometimes badminton but we always returned to our basic game—cricket.

But sometimes, we got tired as well.

When we got tired, we talked. We talked big stories, brave stories, morale stories but the funny ones would come when Tarzan described rich stories. Even his cooked stories and imaginable fantasies were borderlined.

In his nanni's house at some distant town, maternal uncle have such big heart that his son had asked for a Quartz watch and he got it within a week as surprise. This was his richest form of story.

All stories from all the boys had only one thing to check up: nobody carefully ever tells a story, which has an existing witness among us.

There was one boy Ayan in playing circle as well, a mediocre face known to other mates in the playing team often. An unnoticeable guy who was with us almost everytime but we never paid heed to him because neither he put any effort to be in the team nor we thought to put him in.

One day at the mills ground, he had bowled never more enthralling when he was successful in taking three wickets including mine. After our play, normally we would sit, chitchat a while discussing ahhh! This boy hit eight runs today or that bowl he put was unplayable to Sachin even.

It was kind of a technique to motivate ourselves, making the small talk look grand.

That day boys talked about this guy and a major portion of time was he—Ayan.

I looked at him seriously, he was still quite, sitting in the everyday corner place of his own and listening to the talk as he was not the matter being talked about or he was not the one who did it.

In that brisk pouring sunlight, dawn handling the baton to darkness it was that boy sitting, I perspiring, others gossiping (now on other matters).

That face had something of his innocent element so proud or was it the dawned tiring moment that I was thoughtful on this mediocre guy.

He went on to his way, leaving the mills ground quietly as if he had that mediocre label stamped and he had a rigor to follow the label.

Cricket in evenings were sky rocketed happiness and school in the morning were ground defying sadness.

The national anthem was highly sung by me at the school everyday, we played our favorite *chiplety* in the breaks and things dulled around in that second half study process.

When I would reach home, I ate chapatti mixed with milk or rice full plate in a farmer's manner.

Faiza hated my eating style and commented, "If ever somebody sees you eating this way, what impressions would it be!"

By somebody, she meant her friends Harpiiiiiinder and Pravaaaaaa.

I had no problem with Faiza's complaint but I had serious problem with Yassar's sister making nitpicks on cricket. Faiza however always showed me the bigger scope of the game.

But it wasn't that she was no trouble-maker to me; I being a little inferior which she regarded as ugly whereas I had my own optimistic view that I was tall, dark and handsome. Nevertheless It would have been all well if she regarded me ugly only in her own perception or far if she reached to an extent she would tell me; but her far reaching extent were her companions—her friends.

She would most of the time in a kidding environment tell, "my friends don't believe you are my brother"

I in reply said to her, "my friends have the same disbelief as well."

The thing I did not understand at that age was; both the statements meant the same thing—'I was uglier than her'

On next moments, she would reverse her palm and match with my hand, "see who is fairer!"

Though she joked on these matters but I took them very seriously. I tried not to come infront of her friends.

Just on those days, a cousin from England told me, "you see Amen, black boys are more favored by girls in the western countries" I got this statement imprinted on my mouth as a savior to the embarrassing taunts.

My father would imply greatness by the way he was treating all of us in this most difficult phase of our lives. In little times, when I sat in the mosque after the prayers and thought about things that were happening and from somewhere these words had been inferred on my mind, "God testifies us in all ways and it's your patience that will be checked afterall"

On next moments, my mind would reach to an unreal thought that—Is dad the God who is checking me in almost all sort of ways? Is all the world setup for me? How grand the thought would be!!

My father had left an entity and his responsibility was back again to create one. He wasn't to be satisfied by a mere shop or something like that. I knew that, dad knew even better, mom knew too but she broke her patience many a times.

Chapter-2

◆

"So what!" said a devil mind that also propelled in me. Things were entangled in mom's suffering, father's trial and sister's dissatisfaction.

Where was I?

I was physically present everywhere, in everybody's turmoil, tension, feelings but emotionally I was all alone, mentally I was blocked. I think my parents had mistaken when he had sent both of my brothers far place to study and I was all alone in nowhere I guess. I had even problems on a simple shopping process, situation would be like I am standing solitude in a stockpile of clothes hanging all over and yet am I confused for what could go well with me. I had always that perplexing element clutched upon me like the nerves in my blood were plated with the strings of confusion.

I had unnecessary questions. I was growing. I realized it more soundly when I was not afraid of being alone at home. Otherwise as a child, I had those fears of unearthly people all around.

Same way, someday I will be dead and sleeping in the grave all alone in the questionnaire of God. Man, they ask deadly, head-out questions!!
What things will they ask and what will I have to say on uncountable matters?
At the moment, I was growing. I had also started listening to news channel which in my childhood, I suspected my father to be nearly insane that he was so afflicted to listen news of all around the globe.

I was still a kid and had long way till I reached death; atleast I presumed so.
If I would have been dead at this moment, I must have gone to heavens.
I was so crystal clear.

For now, I had doubled my pressure as father was getting well into the finances with eldest brother—Sheezan supporting as well.
I was a privileged student and many others were too in the school.
One day when some of my friends came to my home, he saw my father with a cell phone on his hand, he pointingly said to the other, "buddy, see his father is showing his red mobile phone." Those days, mobile had just come into the market for exclusive people, it defined the status of richest, richer and rich respectively to a mobile phone holder, only missed calls taking and giving mobile holder and about to be a mobile phone holder (has applied and will get it in 3 month's time).
I had all of the world's argument that he wasn't showing but it was his habit to have the phone on his hand.

My mom had a big influence with the foreign moreover to the advancements they had achieved. She would give me an example, "It was just one lakh five thousand English people who ruled the minds of crores of people in India" that was a serious influence.

But the funny influence that she had was—a cousin, Adnan had brought a red medicine from England and to whatever the illness was to whosoever, her offering was always the same red medicine for all probable illnesses.

I was sad most of the times.

No emotions of mine had any right in the living world to stop all activities for a second in mourning for that this boy in this corner is sad . . . very sad. The world had its own pace set over things and if ever all activities stopped for a second, I wonder would have the world been able to run for another second.

Though God was the final taker but he had so much empowered this specie called humans on all matters that we were the masters in this earth. Yes, we are the masters!

In school, after days of practice, senior pro-acticsm, there was the annual function and one of the very reputed and admirable person happening to be the CEO of an institution had come to the school as the chief guest. As all the chief guests were addressing something to us, he also was to do the same thing.

He came to the podium and what he spoke that day was a hint to catastrophically change my life.

He did not start in the regular way as just previously the energy and resources minister had done—I was at this this pitiful phase of life but I came out being this this in my life and the other usual stuffs.

But this man started, "Many people ask me you have achieved so much and you are still perspiring for more, is this not enough?"

And he replied his own question, "I say no because I have been privileged all my life in all matters, school, clothes, home, toys . . . I've got everything.

If I don't reach to that success point, it would be unfair and injustice to what I have got from God to all the other unprivileged people."

That was it and my calf muscle shook for a while, I felt the coldness in my body and my heart knocked—did you get something?

I was so much privileged as well, I have all things in life though my parents have been in little bad times but they never let me come and enjoin them into the hard times.

I have continued the same school and joyfulness has ever been more in this new place with so much of play. I am in a situation that walking to school looks to me as if I have got one of the world's deadliest disease and so am all the time highlighting about this to myself.

People really compare themselves from what they were and not from what others are.

My father had come down from selling potatoes to an industrialist all in his own terms; God being on his side, so it is for this reason that he never feels lowly because he knows where he has come from and he is still above a potato seller.

His speech somewhat summed up on a note for what he had become was a matter that he had to become with so much responsibilities added due to the privilege.

He ended with a quote—Even joy becomes a burden when you can't laugh.

I thought too much over this statement but I could mesmerize nothing else than the face of my maths teacher who had villain smiles to offer when he beat us on all kind of matters and reacted as if he was a soldier and he had done a great nation's pride work by killing an enemy.

I wasn't able to absorb much else than that smiling face but I knew it had stronger meaning.

He walked out of the arena and I gave my friends the exactly same reaction as this—"Oooo what has he said man!"

And the idiot one beside me with spectacles thought it was a question and started explaining me in study terms, "if you study well, you will get everything, but if you don't . . ."

It was a common habit those days to link up things with study matters.

I said to my eldest brother for what he said in the speech but I wasn't able to explain him exactly at that age.

I ran to mom very happy and it was to this day, I found mom had great writings of shayari in a notebook given to her by my grandpa who was a barrister.

She read out on my request the first shayari in Urdu, a different role I had never perceived from her-

Aaj burham ho rahe ho tum meri aawaz ko
Tarsa karoge tum isi awaaz ko . . .

Ofcourse It was not my cup of tea to understand this, then she told me the meaning—Burham means anger; and so I nearly understood all.

I read out the same shayari hungrily to a senior friend at the mosque after namaz. As I was explaining him about what it meant and all else, until then we had been very late in the mosque premises. We were caught up by the jamatis—these were a group of people from different parts of the world to convey people to be good on Islamic grounds. We all were aware that if you stay long in the mosque, you may get caught up by these people.

Yes, we used the term 'caught' as a policeman catches, the same way these people caught.

They would approach very kindly because that was the element they were conveying—"Be good" and almost nobody refused to sit with them for 5 minutes or so and listen to what they had to say.

This time as I was explaining this guy the shayari, who also happened to be a regular sitter with the jamatis after the night prayers. As my explanation got too much jumbled up and was perplexing both of ours mind, he very invitingly and craftily, making it plain and simple said, "hey buddy we will discuss this later, let's sit here for 5 minutes and listen what these people say!"

He knew what these people talked and with a secret mission, he was motivating me as well.

I said – come on let's see then . . .

This jamat was from some different corner of the earth, they had different accent as well.

One of the guy who was standing and speaking about many things, on the line he narrated an incident, he said, "When our group was leaving for the tour, one man eyes closed came to us and said excitedly, Hey friends I came to know that you people are going on jamat so please pray for me to God."

One replied, "Surely we will but what specific?"

The man opened his eyes with the help of his hand, "you see my eyes closed; God just left out to make that spring which helps eye shutter up and down."

I still remember the narrator's pronunciation upppp and dowwwwn as if he had given a world's eternizing wisdom. I crunched, "oh! God"

I felt the minutest organ visible and invisible pronouncingly settled; as if every tiniest particle tickled its presence and said, 'see today you realized me!'

I had seen all that in the bloody biology classes but it meant not which bone was present where, because everybody had those things but here I was, somebody explaining a probable error that could have been in the formation.

This day can be named as 'story day' eventually. My sister also narrated a story following the jamati's story when I shared this with her, she storied with a viewpoint that she could tell me even a nicer one feeling envied that I was uselessly praising a simple story but really it is what you perceive from simple and idiotic things that makes you different.

"There was a blind boy who was begging with a board—I'm blind. People gave him alms, on the line came a man and rewrote the board—Today's a beautiful day but I can't see it"

It was from some of her forwarded yahoo emails.

But my sister for a moment had transformed herself as the best narrator in the scene, so much of drama in her face like an old mother from a movie settling the son's mind so convincingly. My only complaint was that, the story was too short and she did not have that punching vivacity in the signifying line. I could have laughed at the mightiest but the impact she put on me was almost so significant.

Rian had not listened to both of the stories that I had encountered to this day. My class teacher always preached, "where you be at times stand out too important." From teacher's angle, she put that in our minds so we ought not to leave her class but we thought that her classes were taking up our time uselessly, so we took her preaching but just not her way.

Here, Rian indifferently called me downstairs to his room. I attended his call to find an amazing game that he had brought, 'The game of Life'

The game of life was the name of the game and the reason I call it amazing is because, when he displayed the game's outer box he also revealed that whatever happened in this game was to happen in real life also.

We dared not to play it ordinarily.

Later in the evenings, when I would sometimes go to my old house after namaz to the aunties and if haplessly, my brother Sheezan was present there, I would be an entertainer there.

On some matters, aunty would prove me the culprit and I shall be thundered to eat pickle as a punishment like a parrot. The aunt who was a natural born enemy for me, maybe thought I was some inhuman creature and I didn't had the pain in my tongue when I masticated those pickles in between tooth.

I looked that fatso aunt from all corners of the eye, reminiscing all the vengeance relating titles—*Bees saal baad, Pyaasi aatma, badle ki aag* and most importantly 'Murder'

As the pickle withdrew its pain, I gave a damn for what happened.

I didn't mind doing these things now because I had understood that these were little trials and tribulations of life that was very small comparing to the sufferings that other people had.

I was really very mature at that age and my mom had her golden teachings bestowed on me all the time not directly but her acts always inspired me.

What better life could I be living into where my father was so much inspiring and mother doing the same.

I always had a blaming point that my brothers were sent outside the country to study but I was left alone here in this small city but when I realized; what they were missing not being here, I knew what I was to achieve.

As to now, what I had achieved at this age was options.

I had all kinds of life calling. I thought to be a cricketer when the world cup had approached and every soul was mingled in the humdrums of the game and so I thought, 'I will be that big banner guy someday' or sometimes I thought of becoming a scientist when I came to know that Albert Einstein and people like Newton were also idiots in their schooling time, sometimes a laborer and live a small life with hand to mouth lifestyle when I saw a movie of Amitabh Bachhan quoting, "happy life is here and not in the buildings" or sometimes even a businessman when I read stories of man from nothing to everything.

With situations, I had all kinds of life calling.

I thought, I had really lots of options but when I progressed with age, the options minimized and I from rocket scientist to blankness.
However positive I spoke, one's hard time is really a hard time and every problem's staunchest feature is that it looks as if that's the biggest problem.

I had my own problems as well though mom said it was nothing to other people's comparison but then a problem was a problem.
In school, our vice principal would be out after the lunch in all classes to find students who were sweating a lot assuming that he had played a running game. Any kind of running in the school premises was like a criminal who will surely get caught up in the fifth period.

I knew the crime so I almost tried and never did it but I and Sunil had no sweating reasons. Whenever he would be on checks, sometimes we ourselves didn't know which part of our shirt was wet but vice principal would find out so we were always the one to get the severe beating on the bumps.
The boys who actually played the running game would giggle and so I would realize why justice statue is blindfolded.

I felt to complain very strongly against this but I and Sunil were both poor students and poor students were like 3rd class citizens in our school.

When we were out of school after the day-off, with a flavor of vengeance; I often tried and brought a situation to ask the other mates; Hey! Did you 'trim' your nails or do you brush 'twice' a daily?

To whom I put this question would look my face dumbstruck because the usage of 'trim' and 'twice' were exemplarily new words and the boy would look to answer in the shortest way possible feeling inferior and fearing what if more of such questions is thrown!! Who knew, I also only had two sophisticated words in my wallet at that time!!

Everybody's ambition was to become something but my ambition was to be big, a grown up.

I didn't know what I would have become but I knew with so much on mind, I was sure to become something with the will of God.

My mom had said, "There is one moment you will be able to measure and evaluate your life completely over what you have achieved and lost in actual.

It will be the moment when after judgment day, you will be legalized for heavens and then you will be once taken to the hell's site to see what you have escaped from and finally achieved. The same way, when the hell becomes legible upon, you will be taken to see the heavens site and there's no bigger loss than that"

There was so much truthfulness in her say but practically we were so untouched by the things that were to come.

My mother confirmed, "This is a promise by God"

I supposed myself a different person than the rest but there was no evidence supporting the seeming fact. Very quickly, it was disheartening to find almost every second person presuming that they were different beings than ordinary people, I could never comment on them.

Self proclaimed 'different' people were so many that as if the ordinary people were now the different ones.

I used to see in television, some were mercurial talented in their studies and one day they proved out being a hero to every human being on earth; or some were total idiot and proved the same; or some were so innocent that they were embraced with supernatural powers and so these people were actually different.

I was no were different if I had to conclude myself as a religious follower of those sitcoms.

Yes, but I was an idiot but that too not in high spirits as Einstein so I probably lacked this field as well.

Soon I consoled myself, I was no different rather you could find me in the most ordinary collection of people and apparently upon stating this, most of the people would think reflecting in their face that 'this man is something else!!' When I received those reflections, it was satisfyingly good.

This was a time when I found that all the spectacle wearing boys had friend of the same kind. Good students favored being a friend of a good student, bullying boys liked befriending the same category, no-complicated people liked befriending their batch of people.

This thought knocked on my mind when I feared khurram, Yassar, Tarzan also would go far from me because I was not the one like them. I had a watch, an organizing capability and at situations I could add up everybody's 2-rupee myself alone. I was not of their type.

I had expressed my pity over the sun—'the yellow fireball' that Faiza had taught in the rickshaw was so bright but it was very far and solitude. I never wanted to be alone and I knew if ever I had a companion it was only to be Faiza but she also didn't had the chunk to be my friend because she had better companions I guess.

It was a part of time when I was literally searching for a friend. In the school premises, I watched everybody deep down in 10 years; would they be friendly with me without any conditions.

In the mills ground, I watched everybody's eye crystal clear; would anybody from here clutch my hand as a friend forever?

I had made most of my principals as a child, sheezan always said that people change when they grow up—from the time they are out of their mother's womb they find change and with a bursting laugh he stated, "this is the reason why a child always comes out crying in this newer world.

Everyday something is changing, every moment eye is shifting and change gets witnessed."

I had a conflicting view with my eldest brother for his misinterpretation over matters. He had a habit of interchanging words like failureness and incompetency to greatness and sacrifice.

My interpretation over things were simple, why accept the wrong change!!
I think my search over a friend was raging towards to be destined in the mills ground when we were playing relaxingly.

Ayan had the guts to come and sit beside me as if he knew what I was searching and also he knew that it was he who had to be the destination of this small search.
He today not only had the guts to sit beside me but also ask me—Amen, why you not playing today?
I said, "not feeling well!"

Later 2-3 days, almost the same way, each day he sat beside me.
He said to me one day, "you don't know what I have missed in life." That was the day when I decided to clutch him as my friend for the rest of living.

A boy with no parents from early age
He was called by an orphanage home to live with them but he had decided to be on his own so they had remunerated it with studies. He was studying with the help of good people. I think he was broadly strong person away from the body builders advertising of what they had made all day in the gym.

He moved as well to another city in another orphanage for further studies. He was lost too until some years later when I was to meet him.

Ayan arrives in later part of the novel

Chapter-3

*A*fter 8 months we were in our house, our own semi completed house just enough for us to encapsulate inside. We had shifted from father's friend to our own home. In the mean time, I had reached 9th standard, 3 months left towards the end of the session. Things were like a turnover as my memory shifts into our new house. Rian was still a good friend but I had never gone into the mills ground any day back again after I was deadly sick with typhoid and upon coming back home from hospital, I saw those pennies being collected from house wardrobes literally to pay clinical fees for a sum of twelve thousand and some hundred rupees.

School days were still ugly for me, everyday when I woke up the scent of books and the school air was constant on my nose as if somebody had settled an enemy on my nostrils but doing whatsoever I had to engulf in the air that was settled all around.

Adolf sir, the vice principal would hit on my bumps for that I sweated a lot on checks.

I always had the same question on mind though I have phrased it now that what's a worth going to school if I don't enjoy this part of life!

The same strictness, pipe beating on my bumps, same mathematical enigmas, same pitiful looking face to be made in the optional classes as I had made the drama to save myself from very severe beating by the ruthless teacher.

The teacher had known quick time by sources that I had made a drama and yes drama was totally unorganized, it had no even spaces of telling the next fake to support. Drama that I still had little pain in the stitched area of appendices operation that had taken place 3-4 years back now. I felt supreme infront of the friends for the fakeness that I had made, but they funnied and that ruthless teacher patronized in himself as if he had known a dead jewel thief's address and so he clutched on me everytime. I also knew that he was a knower of my fakeness but I had no idea of confessing rather I would all the time make him more rattled with the thought that I had dramatized a lie. So he had once clearly uttered infront of the whole class that he would not 'let me go upper grades'

I grew excited because now a challenge was on my back. I always had the fact in my mind that to be different you got to have tasks different than others.
I had a different task but its direction was quite simple because now the maths world ruler-teacher had also not so clearly specified but hinted that I was not gonna go forward with the grades.

There was no doubt that I was exceptionally poor in studies. I did not like where I was, what I was becoming. I had same opposing attitude towards school as every other student had but however bad they spoke about school, they would distrust me and go on passing the monthly tests, within the same group some got first, some got second and there would be very few companions really accompanying me in the failing section.

I had never put in any serious thoughts over the direct and indirect promises by the teachers. Just then I came to know by my failing companions that they had found a way out.

On inquiring all about, I got to know that they had double tuitions now from the optional and the maths subject teacher both.

They were now assured of being pass not on the grounds that they would study but that they would get help behind the scenes.

I was also advised to do the same but I grew lazy to follow the very time I heard of the planning. Lazy because it needed to put a lot of effort to go and say sorry to both the teachers for the rude and guiltless attitude, then I would be enjoined in the same unethical arena to get pass. The upmost fear, the most intriguing was that upon my proposal for the tuitions, what if they refuse to take me in; I would be the loudest blot of rotten meat in the premises that I hate the most.

Though I later realized that those teachers also expected me to join the tuitions but then I grew even more clear that I wasn't joining.

One day as I and one of constant failing companion was coming out of the school very late, who by the way was also threatened by teachers that he shall not be upgraded shared something of him. He started telling what the consequences would go in his home as the after failing effect.

I first time trembled up within . . .
Oh shit!!
I have a link too—"my home"

All my coolness, hippy attitude and show-off infront of friends 'so what if I fail, I'll still be me' kind of attitude blew away at once to the frightening masters.

My standard at looking things were my brothers. I never wore spectacle because none of my brothers had ever put in.
I then just concerned myself that none in our brothers had even failed.
My father who was so respectable everywhere; what if somebody came to know that his son has failed!
Those were to be the after-effects of my failing.

Exams were near and the fate was getting clear.

Football world cup came up too on the same line, I would know what were team's tactic in all matches then what were mathematical formulas.

I sensed that my ego was far too behind to face all the consequences but now I was very late for the tuitions as well.

My sister was also as poor as me in studies but she had a good behavioral record which was half enough to pass her.
On rickshaw, I would save almost 4 rupees on those days by walking a long distance to school and stopped again for a long walk before going home.
But when on few days my sister was to be taken with me, I could make her walk after the school pretexting that rickshaw isn't ready to go from here but I could pretext nothing as to make her walk before coming home.

She knew my acts but I loved all those faces from her. I would often buy her chakufrom the vendor because it looked as if you got very much for just 1 rupee.
I would save that money because I knew mom had hard time saving those bugs to give me everyday for rickshaw.
It was so hard at times that though I knew she loved me to an extent, but she did not mind if I walked the whole distance from school to home.

From all those pitying matters to reality matters was contrasting.
What was all money saving and sacrifices meant if I was to disappoint my parents in the most matterful way!
I never studied at home. I woke up before school and did all the essential homeworks: very essential homeworks only. Those would sometimes be enough to exempt me from the punishments but sometimes it didn't.

I was seriously being expelled in my thoughts to do something but with immaturity, I didn't know how much mind I really did have because I had no much closest of buddies, nor any brothers with me.

Yes, I had one elder brother-Sheezan at home but didn't matter at all because however far or near he stood to me; our distance was constantly the same.

Final exams had come in to the line, I studied just the night before as my usual setup on a hurrying mode and luckily say or unluckily most of the time, one of my brothers would be at home and I was made to study the whole night.
I didn't study but I showed that I did.

I would go play our chungi game similar to cricket after the exams sensing that I would fail but also I behaved like an ostrich who when sees a hunter, digs the hole quick and puts her face inside; thinking that now the hunter is out of the sight.
And on the next moment, the ostrich gets a thaaaaaaang on her ass.
I was avoiding the view that I would fail but it was almost like imminent for me to fail.

Mom's first question as I stepped inside the house would always be the same in a querulous tone with lots of doubt flavored in it, "How was your exam son?"
Never did my exams went bad from my point of view and if it had gone dreadful then my point of view always shifted to the teacher—ahh he is very kind and likes me . . . so he'll pass me afterall these people do realize what failing means for a child.
But all emotionalizing thoughts went in vain when results were out; even though I always had flicker of optimism left that those were just terminal exams and it is the final where one has to clear up.

I was scorching to the upper grades somehow but this part of ninth class seemed now was the time to get trapped.

The results were out, I don't remember what sources made me know about the results.

I had failed!

I hit a woman with bicycle; she crouched in the middle of a road, who cares!

The cycle that I got as a child was lost somewhere in the moment, that wasn't a big deal too and who cares!

But I failed, suddenly everybody cared!

I tried and shifted my thoughts to many other things but I was inaccessible.

I ran, ran and looked around for where I was heading to. I trustfully lent my brain to legs for wherever it took me at this point of time except home.

I ran towards the city boating area to completely change my perception atleast for this day.

"First moments are always empty"—were the words of an Olympic gold medalist out of sheer excitement and jubilancy.

"Then you sit down, plan things, decide what to do next and go forward with it"

I could sit down for hours, yet come out planning nothing, deciding nothing and nothing to go forward with.

The first moment was empty and the emptiness hadn't yet ceased!!

I was blank.

Just as I was blank almost nothing on my mind except the view to which I was seeing—the boats coming and going.

To a far-off distance, I saw a ship totally still in the sea. It was about to reach the shore but now it had stopped due to a sudden gust.

After my own line of predictions, the ship moved well and reached the shore.

The wayfarers boarded out and with them exited the head of the ship. I was quite anxious to know something of that I just saw, what exactly had happened!

I went nearer and the man spoke to his colleague with a sigh, "How relaxing is it to reach the shore!"

I puzzled myself—How relaxing!

"After reaching here—got to go home and get the beating of father," I tried to make it funny to ease-out myself.

I had no guts to ask because on the back of my mind, I was guilty of something-nothing related with the wayfarers but still I felt gutless.

Sometimes doesn't it happen that when we are guilty it seems as if the whole world knows about it and what may we answer if a question is thrown up!

I went again to my cozy clayey seat in the corner to try and continue with the expedition.

It had been long time since I was sitting here but now it started to itch—How long?

How long could I be not going home?

On my quick finish-off with the running idea, just before the move towards home, my heart pinned stunningly towards a quote that I had studied in the arena of useless school

"A ship is safest at the shore but then it is not made for that."

Ahh..!
It was the whole day's payment. How did I get that on my mind. I felt ecstatic.
It was not the ship on the shore-it was Amen.

It was me standing in the shore under the guardianship of father, to the safest of sides.
But, I am not very sure if that is all what I am meant for.

Maybe I am to be with father for my whole life, but I got to check myself with the standards of the world. For where do I stand!
I could not all my age keep listening to stories of people who had tried something big and that we had become so intrinsic part of their inventions.
I eye not to create something new but to enjoy that's been created.
Creation is no creation without its lovers

After hard thoughts, I decided to go home; afterall how long could I be running?
The fact was in my mind that the time I spent will never be back at any cost and this made me fearful thinking what can be done in such a short spanned life that even thinking about time . . . leaves you time behind whereas,

the other collection of thought said everything could be done but many people as me didn't know 'how'

These thoughts are a normal miniature picture in every of our minds and why not; it is too very obvious.
Great ideas come to our mind at most ordinary times and so it just looks like one more link of an ordinary chain but when it's refined and rethought, it starts coming out from the shells of ordinarism.

I was now setting my mind for whatever I do should be remarkable. I wanted to prove and show everybody in this world that here lives a man called Amen or not rather that I die quietly in some unknown part of the world. Dissatisfied with everything at the last moments of life, thinking probably much more could have been done.
People come and go but it is the things they do in life makes an impact, leaves a history behind.

That day the air blew in a very different way.
I had never engulfed the same usual 24 hour around us matter-air so different. And I could guess up the reason as well, afterall air was also one of the innumerous matters under the control of God and all thoughts being developed on my mind was a circumstance being created. Created for what..!

Me?
It was my self-astonishing mode. I was liking it, maybe I also could be in the path of being sculpted or getting intrigued in anywhere to an alumnae of great known people even after they were gone.

Do I have to give a reason for embarrassingly showing teeth in a lonely arena?
Laugh this time was to a thought that, am I hiking things too far all that on a guessing note?

Yes, my mom had said it right—any problem looks as if that's the biggest problem, the most major one.
And that happens to be the most staunching feature of a problem.

There was no written script for my life that I could have read and easily followed neither was there any barometer or a rod to put in a hole and see how much of reality my thoughts hold!

Ahh that air, was I not telling so much under the most indifferent but different air.
Sensuously things were being told and maybe this was the moment when I was realizing that I had some dreams for myself: Whatever be that!
I had seen people around me tight with their schedules and in the limitations of their boundaries majorly reasoning that they are now family-men.
Whereas, I was still single; an individual and I knew that there can be no other better time to fulfill for whatever I have got on my mind but . . . I had nothing on my mind whatsoever that I should have been fulfilling.

Suddenly, I stroke to the words of my weak old uncle reciting in his own language: Experience teaches us more than we expect.
Certainly, none of my uncles were a character to be admired of but I believe that even a thief has something to

teach us about or has the power to change you. Everybody has a little power to inspire others, or if still nobody is inspiring, it becomes dead necessary to have the correct inspiration from whatever we see.

In the ancient ages, pirates what we know as the robbers in the ocean travelled in small boats and looted big ships in the midst of the water jungle. They travelled in such small boats that they had to pick the most necessary items that they required for themselves, they did not loot each and every item but picked the materials wisely so that their small boats did not weigh heavy, threatening their safety. Yes, such should be our idea to life: Pick the inspirations wisely, that is good and suitable to us. Be that man good or bad, anybody can teach us anything. A man might have the lowest of deeds but it isn't necessary that he would do everything wrong.

So, man as a whole isn't an inspiration but his correct ideas are.

On all that note and taking my uncle's word as a pretext to start my journey, I was seemingly strangled by a force to leave home.

Had it been "I" listening all these philanthropist sounding words from someone else's mouth, I would have tried my best to make it funny but when words get thrown by ourselves how valuable do they seem. It feels bloodily sentimental; why aren't you moved by me? Such is my pain in words . . . why don't you get it?

Wow!

I was walking back home with all great encounters that I had made to this day but as I heard my own trample of feet walking, I looked down at my feet and saw the lust dominance of green grass in between the settled pebbles, the assimilation of grass and pebbles had a very brutal message to convey.

I grasped to starkness that 'I was heading towards home' where possibly dad must be waiting with hands moisturized, mom must have leased the morose appearance on her face from the sullen and death looking environment that must have taken all over the house—Faiza must have given the news.

When I was three houses away from the doorsteps of my home, the darkly tinted lights, the unusual empty streets and the grave silence in *mohalla* today looked for a different purpose. There was bitterness airing from some house, there was happiness on my failureness from some house, there was grief from some house and there was jealousy paid-up from some house. I had some remonstrance to present against God, because he was the only one listening without any answer and arguments.

I was afraid to enter inside. I recognized fear at that time.

I was about to meet an entire new father.

My father on his many talks with mom had storied his reason for growing big. My grandmother had explained to him in his youth that there are some acts that a person does which becomes his identification to life.

We call that catastrophic event.

This failing was my first of catastrophic event.

Ever since the process of studies and culture of schooling was started in the history of human being, administrator's way of categorizing students in the borderline of marks was transpired, parent's concern on humanity of no value for their children and scoring of all the value, since then this act to fail in my grades was written.

This was to be my identity as well as destiny.

Chapter-4

Trailed by my thoughts to the ongoing scenario

I had failed!

It came as a simple unusual news but everyday it grew bigger, every then and now it ceased my blood at moments, every minute it shouted on me "this is what you have grown different in" every hour it peeped from some corner, "which grade did you reach" everyone felt superior infront of me.

The sun scorched harder, the wind blew stronger, father colder, mother confused, brother 'what did you do' and I numb.

With the news of my failing, there was also news of people getting passed. Hard to digest were not the friends, but a cousin: Amra

She had been a companion in studies, we had deliberately shared our whole material to talk as sometimes 9.2 exercise 31 question is world hard or Lord Ullin's daughter was the most fascinating poem and else things. Whenever we met, we talked about studies and books and all those in-trend matters for us. It was certain but suddenly with seclusion, she had slipped ahead in the grades and how happy would her parents be on the so-called achievement of their daughter being ahead of me.

I could only immaturely cry over what I had done, consciously in a lonely room. Father went to the school and tried if I could pass anyhow but they weren't ready to take me up because I had almost grown an ego in them for me not to pass.

Dad and Sheezan came out of the school premises. In the van where I was sitting next to the driver seat thinking dad and brother must have convinced them to take me up to the grades. I was praying only if dad could have turned things around this time but apparently it wasn't the only time; brother said which I remember as the most touching moment of my life with him.

He said—'Amen'

I didn't turn my head towards them. I was not legible to have an eye with my dad or brother who were sitting at the back seat.

I was waiting with frozen stare at the front to hear that one lasting good news of my life.

On that 16 and some half years of my age, I had never thought so much all at the same moment.

Sheezan frantically asked, "How would it be studying a one more year in this class?"

Bingo!!

This one line asking moment is what I remember as the most intimate moment with my brother.

A question had never gone so emotional, it was as if the ask itself said 'I know brother what grief you are in but this is only we can do!'

This line was echoing In the van, tears unready to blossom, smile loosened to loss, body hair prickled up, droplets of sweat under armpits, eyes shuttering upppp and dowwwwn like the narrator's voice in the mosque, Soul saying the heart: have no worries buddy!

I stuck my eyes front yet I was able to make a picture of father's face, Sheezan's inner's innest feeling, hoping the driver isn't understanding these high level literate's matter.

I hadn't been in such grief as this one, it was as if I had died and the soul picker had well taken permission from the family. I had no tears for that moment because it would have only been a bonus certification of the failureness if it had come out.

The moment brother asked me this thing, I had my thoughts shifted. I thought about the content of the letter. The letter that I would write, when I run from home because there was seemingly nothing better to do.

Sheezan and dad were discussing and I was scripting my letter

"Dad thankyou very much for whatever I have got from you! You played your role as a parent and now as an adult, it's my role to play.

I as everybody will live a 60-70 year life hopefully. It is said 'time is precious' and it really is; I don't want to live *in the humdrums of scoring marks and tantrums of my ever-changing mates who slip ahead of me in the grades so silkily. Cranium's capability isn't to be judged by the marks I score.*

I will be back someday when I will prove myself. Now I don't wanna be a burden, I don't know what I will do or where I will reach but I am telling you, I will be back."

I was thoughtful for what things would I be going through in an unknown part of the world, when I would be out of the secured parent's shade.

I was excited with the idea of being verily alone with no responsibilities, with no pressures.

My life would really start from zero and even if I reached to a one-level then also it would have been an achievement from my part, whereas I was right now in some 4-5 level from where if I go down, it was a disgrace.

My pursuit for happiness could all change, otherwise upon reaching to an age when I shall be a story-teller to my grandsons, I could only be sighing that I was a good cricketer but I couldn't forward myself in that line. I was a principled guy but I lost them all to my brother's argument that 'nobody remains the same'

Where is the right to live 'my' life gone?
Why are we non-materialistic only in the philosophies?
Give me a space to fall, why always success!

I knew life could be a hell if you are not happy with what you are doing.

Dad had a very good habit as to always say thanks to God for the food he had howsoever it was made because it was one of the ways God came to us and said 'live on'

The letter was scripted and constructed with correction many a times, place suffixed for where I would have left it, reactions assumed of all the people but I never wrote it in fair handwriting for two reasons-

One, I never ran from home.

Second, I feared if dad would even understand my handwriting as it was so bad though I thought to get it printed but that wouldn't have tong the emotional strings audible.

However, the core reason that I never left home was my mom. I don't know how would have she reacted but from my side I would have only added up the grief and pressure to find me up when they themselves were so much in pressure of the business.

The cry seemed endless to me and I knew it was to be a catastrophic matter, more powerful than the chief guest's speech, a label on my head for the rest of my life.
Things I knew were to change . . . I had failed man! A worse thing seemed that I knew all the happenings and I had no weapons at all . . .

What next would it be for me now, I didn't know at all because father was the decider of my fate though it was all written on the cards but the in-form decision taker appointed was he.

When God made this world, ever before human existence he made a thing called Pen and ordered it to write. The pen asked, "Oh Almighty What to write?"

He said, "Write all people's fate"

And yes . . . at that moment, my fate was written too. What was written on my life.

I had little dear savings but I could give all if someone could articulate me my steps from here on.

I had no clue at all over dad's reaction

Uncle would sometimes come home and be equally surprised everytime on the matter that I have failed, "Oh, he couldn't pass. I wonder what will he be able to do in further stages of life?"

This uncle was a man who cared of nothing because he got nothing on his own. For him, any talk with the company of laughter could go no wrong and to a listener, it just gave a hint of casualness with the backdrop of too much sarcastic seriousness.

His reactions would be something like, "oh he failed" though he knew things well off and still showcased as if you have failed in the easiest part of life and he was the most concerned one regarding my future.

Did God have choices when he created this world?

If there was, how was it, how worse was it or was it a personal choice of God to put us in these situations?

Ok fine!

I don't complain for what God put us into or to the hard times that I am into, but the biggest problem is: We just don't know when we are failing and when we are struggling.

The world's language had changed.

Humanity was only a spoken word, a lofted delusion.

I don't know what noble or wicked thing might have I done being in dad's place. But what he did was an exemplary act from him towards me.

I was made to continue the same school with ever more facilities and with ever more conviction and motivation.

In the march of 2001, I started with the repetition of the same class in the same school.

Time passed by and I surrendered myself to different tasks.

By the time of Eid on December 17, time had long gone I hadn't gone to the mills ground any day back again.

After the namaz, I found Tarzan, as always—small man in tiny steps, face certifying the gratification, never ready to leave eyes of the one who he is approaching.

We held greetings to each other and I was so happy to see him—one of the members, we would always be worried to find on the match days.

What our family's reputation had been was very respectful and financially well above the other families in the *mohalla* though internally financial matters had slacken now. I put hands inside my pocket, churmured the notes and brought out a 10 rupee note and presented to Tarzan. He happily took that and I proudly gave it.

After a long time, I was invited to the field, the old mills playground; kind of a reunion of our *mohalla* cricket team. The play was good again, the very same way we did everything but now, I knew things were not to be as regular and routine as it used to be.

Tarzan had come to play in a blue formal shirt, loose enough to conceive 'trying to be a gentleman' needful as it looked for a man completely immersed in a goggles store unlike old days when his pockets were filled with amusing stuffs from peeping comb in the back to cosco ball in hand showcasing his ready to play attitude anytime. I was travelling to the good old adventurous days of time travelling history contrasted to my ridiculous delusion of present.

Khurram wearing his own tailored cotton pant to which I prefer saying 'bribe' but his father had placed it as a 'gift' upon Khurram's decision of accompanying him in the tailoring shop fulltime now. The dirty clothes were replaced. My grey tracksuit had no much ways of seeing those old playful Saturdays.

Chapters in life has slow opening and hurried endings.

My senior once said to me, "life is like a bicycle, keep pedaling"—I said okay.

Someone else said, "life is like an ice-cream, enjoy it before it melts"—I said okay

Another someone said, "Life is a hollow space"—I said okay

Sometimes I had to even inquire, "Are they all talking about the same life!"

My father was a man of possibilities, white skin; it looked as if the sun's ability of making the skin tan had never approached this man coated with a well groomed urdu language on his tongue.

He gave my invaluable lessons when he sat and talked to mom on various matters. One evening talking to mom he said, "A man from south sent a telegram to two different jungle tribes head asking; I am a small shoe manufacturer and I want to know if there is possibility, I can start shoe trading here.

After quite a time, from one of the tribes, reply came, "it's useless . . . nobody wears shoe here."

And the other tribe head replied, "Great opportunity . . . no one has ever wore shoe here"

This kind of definitions ruled his mind where he captured probability over impossibility. He was a hard-working man.

After I had failed, life's only definition was my personal experiences.

I started liking darkness, isolated from all, nobody seeing me, me watching none, no questions, no answers, walking lonely with shade, these were the things that I was liking sub-consciously.

Though my optimism part of thought never left me—it could be simply God's testing; if people could spit on the prophet and even crucify some, that too happening to be tests of God then who was I to be depressed on such a small thing. After all, cranium's capability is not a dividing factor among humans.

Why is everybody so adamant on pointing out to the mistake that I have made!

Has God not promised to give sufferings only to a level that humans can endure?

On that evening I drew my first serious meaningful sketch on a tissue paper, a picture that contained my frustration of me being left out.

Me stretching hands, wretched, distressed in a railway platform pledging my friends to stop the train for that I was left out, but No! They did not care to stop and forwarded themselves to the upper grades.

Here I was standing alone inside the picture, outside the picture, all taunting to their best—now that they have got a chance for this boy who talked so big.

Everybody laughing at the loudest they can. When God created Adam and Eve after lots of evolution in the world, he created as many species in the animal kingdom but only one species in human kingdom with one staunching feature: humanity.

There was no humanity in any of the faces who had boarded on the upgraded train.

Why has success' definition succumbed on being pass everytime and to keep walking constantly the way other competitors are walking?

Did mom mean nothing when she said that the achievement quotient from life can be measured only when you will be entering the heavens and God takes you to see the hell's site?

Let me be out of the competition, let me get into the thorns so strongly that I become able to realize the stage when I reach the rose petals.

Let me fail a couple of times, the thorns annealed in my body and when I get out of it, let me realize this is how it feels to be good.

This is the reason why a homeless beggar's most satisfying moment is when he gets a hut and this is the reason why an emperor suicides his life on being degraded to a succumbed palace.

But all I talk big and wisdom is no means to get out of what shameful I had done.

Though I had known the value of life from my point of view but my viewpoint shivered whenever somebody asked, "Which class are you in buddy?"

How difficult was it to answer, I knew the question would be thrown from whosoever but never had I got the scripted lie ready.

I do remember when I got late for school on an examination day and dad dropped me to school in the van half an hour late.

I hurryingly paced to the examination room and the incharge came looking after me because he had to file up a reason 'why was this boy late?'

I with a confused mind plotted a story to them—'I had an accident with a bike' with its detail.

Half an hour later, again the examination incharge came up just to show his rotten detected face complying to me that 'your father had come to the office and has apologized that his son got late because he was asleep till late in the morning'

I was such a dumb or from my view principled that I did not organize the lie in a 30-minute drive with dad for what would we be vowing together infront of the school authorities for our late entry in the examination.

I realized evolution inside me as a liar when my closest buddy Rian, even didn't know exactly what was happening in my exams and which grade was I exactly in.

It was a funny matter when thought over but as only a bald person can feel the heat on his head and for all else it's nothing more than a laughing matter, the very same way I was only the one feeling heat.

My principles were going, the ones that I had so meticulously clutched on for my time of life. It was getting hard for me to follow my-made principles as a child.

Dissatisfactions were many, dilemmas uncountable and so it was that the idea of leaving home was still there. Leaving everything was certainly a good idea then being sullen at home, giving a food for thought to all the home members. Why havoc them when all I did was my act, no others involved in it!

My interpretation alike everything was simple; life is to be lived_____.

The blank was to be filled by us; happily, sadly, religiously, etc. However you lived, it was sure to get over but the regret on your old age discovering that there was a better way to fill in the blanks 'when I was in my youth' is like a small sized brother to the loss that we will see in the face of heaven when we will be taken to the hell.

The inability to go back and live your youth is something indescribable.

My father almost in everything had a quotient to match up: Is he satisfied with what he did or would he regret after a little time?

I knew my dad's act as this one. He used to say, "the inability of doing something is one of the worst things God gives us. A simple sneezing is a way to relax your senses but if that simple activity gives its hint of coming and doesn't come for a minute, it disturbs the whole mechanism.

When it comes, thanks to God for that."

I asked, "Why for such a small and routine thing?"

In one line he answered and shuttered his mouth, "leprosy patients don't have the ability to sneeze."

I was very sad in all spheres of the talking point but music's audacity sounded to me with passion, knocking to the soul and saying 'you are not the only one! why you showcasing as if you are the ambassador to unhappiness, why are you the advertiser of sadness?'

Yes, really I wasn't the only one; many in this world were no-good in studies but still had brilliantly forwarded themselves to living.

My mother often watched Islamic talks on television with which I would accompany her sometimes. A preacher in a usual style was sitting on the couch and with the holy book infront was interpreting worldly and divined matters. He said without looking at the Quran for a while abridging his own philosophical and aged experience—an ant is a small creature. Often humans see, pity and ask what would have God thought to send him down here infront of such huge creations?

The preacher self-answered in a curious tone.

That ant says, "Though I am a small creature, I am the creation of God, working the hardest to live than any of you from the human beings. I go out everyday, exploring a newer world and everyday I struggle and everyday I win because everyday I survive. Though I am an ant, a small creature. When I fight with all kinds of things and come out surviving, I am still living. I am still embracing the beautiful life that God has given us by being happy with what I have got for myself though it's a struggle, though it's a hard-ship but by fighting to make things better, I prove out that I love the life that's been given to me."

I had other things to do in life seriously but all I was into right now were mere time passing activities with blend of dissatisfaction loud and unclear.
With a grand term called life, there is a plot called 'time' as well. Time tickled and life settled.

While we were watching our favorite serial—Malgudi days, I don't know what came in Rian's mind that he queried all of a sudden, "Hey Amen, was it not just 2 year back that we had seen a millennium year?"
I turned my head towards him and at first glance, I tried to laugh.
On second careful, thoughtful glance, I tried to curse him for clicking the realization.
The need to evaluate things were at ultimate call on us. Newspaper's public interest slogan—'Now is the time to act' on women's day wasn't only for women because more than anyone else, I guess it was published in the interest of Amen.

There was a trend that people had to follow at different eras. This era had the trend of chasing your dreams and being self-sufficient, it was a way of proving 'yes, I'm cool enough too'

If I had to evaluate myself, I had thoughts and if those could be converted, I had dreams as well but as if everything was known except what was it.
One of the most troubling elements for people of my age was that, things knocked onto our soul, screeched to get something hard but only that knocking element never told; "who exactly was he!"

It was in rare moments of time that I became so passionate about things but as I tangled up with the same world, in pursuit of living, marching the same audacity of tune that everybody thumped on, the idea would get lost. It would get completely lost even to what I had thought a couple of days back.
Dusk and dawn was yet into at its own time table, the streams still sang their continual song, uninterested and indifferent to the anxieties of the world. I would again reimburse myself to the time when God created world, the first thing that he created was a pen and ordered it to write (The same scripted story) The pen asked, "Oh! Almighty, what to write?"
He said, "Write all man's fate from this point to the point of time the world will end from one's birth to death."

Yes, I was also a part of that writing, that grand writing where it is speculated that life came onto us once, we did things once, we achieved things once but I suppose we didn't fail once.

It was hard to consistently fail in all spheres of opportunity, but I was that hard guy, that stern hard guy, unready to blossom in the shades of exhaustion.

This time, I was failing to hold down my own principles that I had made as a child. Many could simply argue, why not re-model thoughts and aims that you have hoped to become as an adult but I had very strong belief that the first thoughts that came in our minds were the perfect ones.

You may modify it with more and more changes but if you stand incompetent with the world on a certain thing, even though we might give the whole world for whole life a deception, "this is the thing I love to do."

In actual, the happiness that hasn't knocked yet is because it has known that the one who lives beside this door is the one who has feared to attain what has been in his mind to do all his life from childhood.

So, the first ambitions that we make as a child are the finest ones.

Boys in my class had earphones on all the time, reacting as they are the most loving ones carrying the passion of music but on the line, they forgot to enjoy music though the earphone remained as a constant juggler.

Nikita, if I had to evaluate her, she was a gem. A classic in between all of the others with so much of attitude, when I watched her, it looked the world had slowed its pace and that charm of graciousness was for me to explore.

I never dared talking to her except in the utmost need of pen and pencils. But if I ever had to complain God on some matter, it was surely the unstoppable time. Though it looked time had lessened its passing pace but then it was just a deceiver.

On those days, I had seen a play enacted by Sameer and group called 'I failed!'

It was one of the most pride filled play relating in many instances which was presented simply, yet with an enormous impact on mind capturing the philosophy that people who fail are people who live extra-ordinarily, very much corresponding to the philosophy of providing a space to fail.

The useful thing that I could pluck out from the act was that it conveyed that with failing, you have stood out different from others and if you make positive, that difference is good more of a times because you come out tasting that necessarily required bitterly medicine. It summed up on a note, if you haven't failed, you haven't lived.

Life has strange reasons to go on.

Our home maid was a very happy woman though she had no much reason in her livelihood to justify her satisfaction and contentment but then 'she was happy'

Her face was tanned and leathered due to the extra exposure in the sun, cloth possessing a clumsy outfit, three lines on the forehead specifying the tension of her daughter's marriage, cheeks well gone inside, hands toughened and hair withered.

While she washed dishes and mom did other household chores, their talk had an ingredient called "ease-out" which made mom to have a constant smile in the morning. Often I was attracted to talk with her to the fact that she is making my mom happy and it was quite an anxiety to know what's so special charm in her that make things look so easy.

Often I woke up in the morning and it was a usual sight in the kitchen. My part of easing out mom was to make tea for her and in that; my selfish pursuit was to grasp and underline the talks from this maid.

I talked to her waking up many mornings but very quickly, I found that though she had the vivacity, there was no such admirable accent in her talk. In contrast, she sometime sounded very boring and on following days, her talks could be presumed and smiling if it came rarely was for her tireless effort for the efforts she put.

The sufferings that she had in life were an intrinsic part of her everyday living and I guess she did not know how was it living without the pain. The way she was living, was the way she had presumed it to be naturally made by the creator.

She did not know at all about the wantonness in the eyes that people had of jealousy and unfaithfulness. She did not know that not very far from her house' mud flooring, there are people who have glittering marbles and stones sparkled in walking paths. She did not know that there is a culture of spending 'vacations' in holidays, and that holidays were not meant as 'bonus time for childrens to work' She did not know that not very far from her walking feet, there are people who have ravishing dark Mercedes, seated in the upholstery leather. She did not know that not very far from her eyes, there are some eyes which has dreams, aspirations and a possibility with willingness of turning every small thing into big.

She walked a little less than a kilometer everyday in morning and subsequently in the evening to come our home and wash the dishes. Her gas cylinder was still running after seven years due to crucial usage, her husband's attitude was like a desperado and her son's strife continued with the co-workers. Her tiresome effort in cultivating the same mirthful face just hinted if it was all a drama, a mask which she had adorned to get rid of the tedious discouragement that the world could have produced in words if she had given the world a chance through weak attitude shown off.

Witnessing her smiles, masked or unmasked in anyway a factor generating jealousy sought, "If contentment was any of her business to the kind of picturised life she portrayed?"

She was not afraid to confess about the problems through the husband and son's constant fiasco in whatever field they entered. Though she wasn't let-down by her own blood flop-works either.

After many early morning wake-ups, ease-out tea served, I was getting nearer to the maid's contentment.

Whenever she talked, majority of the time, their family's efforts were talked about. She was proud of the suffering and the failures that their family got into almost everytime; it was then I got a click on my mind to a matter of fact that it wasn't actually failing for maid but it was a customization and normalcy in the schedules of her life.

The value of a distant island is only to be viewed perfectly from the eyes of a drowning man.

Here she was—a woman who had permanently settled her life in an island realizing well the absolute isolation.

From my viewpoint, what she was in; was not her failureness but a simple situation of life with which she had been accustomed all her age. Though she stood proud with all things but in a slow motion; she hadn't lost anything, she hadn't been degraded in anyway. There was no person who would welcome the brand 'fail' but it was that they got into it so deeply and then they started praising this brand alleging the failureness element as their focal learning point. It is simply like interchanging words describing traits such as incapability to sacrifice.

It is much easier to see light from darkness but it isn't easy to see darkness from light.

Maid didn't teach any lesson; just that she subconsciously tonged up strings inside me: life has strange reasons to go on. We inspire our falling act and draw an understanding through it only when we have failed, we love many things only when we gone into it.

My friend Rian had no strange reasons but very important decision to make when it came to play 'the game of life'

What if we strike down to pay heavy taxes when the dice don't fall right, what if we fall in a river at some point of the game, and what if we die at the age of 40 in this game.

There were better things to do then seriously think over sensitive issues all the time drilling yourself that you have done this wrong and else.

The better thing that I found was to listen to live musical performance, the music in cassettes and cds were dim compared to the live performances.

It was a song performance 'main ek fard hoon' by my classmates in an inter-school competition. I hadn't caught a song so well phrased up entering my ears amazingly sweet. Next, on the evenings watching 'small wonder' with my sister with round the corner fights were the perfect face of a 'beautiful life'.

Chapter-5

I had been at my best times as well. After more than a year and a half, here I was preparing for my first public examination of class 10.

Everybody did lots and lots of preparation, most of my mates to acquire the topper's badge but I did my whole—hearted preparation to acquire the passing marks.

I and two other good friends stayed in a hostel cum paying guest which was run by a dedicated husband and wife. Those 2 months were the first time I was staying far from mother and family.

We played like monkeys, ate like chimpanzees, comical like idiots.

The two hostel guardians complained so satisfyingly as if they wanted us forever in their little place but it was needful to show that we haven't left you like open bulls, just a small reminder of you are under someone's guardianship.

I and my other two friends twice in a week went for shopping in the evenings; brought about tuna fish cans, ready to eat uncooked noodles and if we had extra bugs we often lingered on the soft drinks; but too very often.

Those were like I was regaining my time back again; the good ones. The sun would see at me and announce in an asking mode: how is it again having beautiful days, son?

I did not have the courage to answer everytime to it because a sentimental string all the time popped up on my head, and this time it was for my undecided factor; what after this schooling part is over? Would such situation of life be forever?

I looked not to concentrate much on that because all these years I had thought to change myself with an extreme need but I hadn't change was the underlying fact. Thus, I was an unchanged man who was living in the moments of flow. If life was to get over all in a sudden obscurity and it had customized itself not to spare even a second moment, then why should I spare so precious capability of the cranium over life's matter.

This was the thing that I also associated studies with; knowledge was no more a knowledge, it proposed the new theory only to pursue a career.

If these were things I told to my friends, they would give me world's argument of my wrongliness. Truly so, had I also been one of those toppers, I doubt might or might not have I taken up things this way.

But here I was; bestowing my certain philosophy to the realization that if we are meant to study for 20-22 years to stand in a better situation of life when we are 35-40. Were things worth it?

I did realize that everybody wasn't sad at the time they were at school so I condensed things just to myself.

Yes board exams had neared to neck, one among the other two hostel-mate was really very talented though he was the wittiest of all but then he was a genius in knowledge. I liked his character and wished if ever could have I also been caught up with traits as this boy, how proudly would have my parents reacted to me!

This was the second moment.
This was my second moment in the walking life that I would ask God in heavens to make me relive back again if he had promised to give everything we ask for. Though there was no number set to ask for in context to reliving moments but I had limited them to myself.

If some philosopher actually jotted down, followed by the script writers and acted by Abhishek Bachhan conquering to the question that living each moment was the thing, and if you couldn't do it, were you still living?
He would have surely been unthoughtful in that flickering moment of dialogue delivery that in some corner lives a boy called Amen hurting the basic thriving existential part of his. I wasn't able to live at my best, though I was majorly the only culprit but then I was not the wholly culprit.

Things were preaching in every instance, the thought of what if I fail again never left its knocking habit on my mind. This fear, if I went through statistics would prove that I was only one out of thousand partners sharing the same tragedy or else some had overcome it so well that they thanked, they had failed in that not-so important time of life.

But a tragedy for one wasn't equally same for the other. Though the tragedy had taken place almost one and a half years back now and I did realize that it was just a simple unusual happening that I had gone through; but then it never made me feel so simple about the whole matter.

I was basically tortured on moments when somebody threw question relating to study stuffs and elaboration seemed to me the hardest job that a person could ever do. Many a times, I landed up with different stories to different people on the same matter.

I laughed at myself sometimes over how I was dramatizing the whole lie and sometimes I wasn't the only one laughing.

I was like screening a 20 inch movie into a 42 mm theatre, I was just hiking things too far then it actually was.

My mother who was a mentor in every step of my acts, she did not inspire or motivate in a very direct style but she had something I believe, had there been any other person apart from me, he could not have grabbed what mom had mostly to say or even mom mightn't have told any other creature.

She had said to me, "a person sometimes does so much of social work, helpful work and so on the line they often come out without checking for what change have they actually been able to administer or what was the impact of the act they performed?"

She described an Iranian movie, 'the song of sparrows'. I had seen this movie alongwith director's two other fantastic movies. I knew the director's way of pivoting the character with blend of so much honesty but I could not have told this to mom because I wanted to hear this movie from my mother's corner. She was like taking me to a different junction catching my hand to show a different angle of the same picture. I knew she had these days the motive of apprising me in all sorts, trying to motivate her son from all odds.

The story involved Karim, a man who lived his life by taking care upon ostrich eggs in the farm. One day eventually as something has to happen, one of the ostrich gets lost for which Karim is held responsible. This way his job was gone. Further in a situation, he goes to the city for repairing hearing aid of his daughter; there in the city mistakenly he is thought to be a motorcycle driver by a peddler ferrying in the busy traffic. Suddenly, he realizes his new job-of that ferrying people in motorbike in the busy traffic.

My mom stopped here, the story had more but she stopped here.

Now, she replayed in a slow motion; that man Karim drank a sip of tea offered from the master alongwith the drip of the news of being fired from the job.

"You know what Amen; life stops nowhere because the fate-writer has meticulously planned for all of us though we think it had happened totally without links. The falling of leaves is a replacement process for the new budding leaves.

The first thing that God made in this world was a pen." Exactly, what I had realized some months back.

Mom continued, "God ordered it to write and he wrote every man's, each and instance happening that he/she was to go through.

This is because God had plans for all of us."

She had totally forgotten on the while that it was Karim's story that she had narrated to me at first as the background scene but I didn't mind listening to what now she had to say.

"Your father had patience and was almost jobless for four years before he made his own industry, a dream that he had cherished.

If people fail in certain things, it is not because the pen stopped writing further plans but it was written too and the irony is that not even the prophets know what's the written stuff!

So the irony demands us to be self-holders of the fate."

She was speaking almost the usual words until this:

"There is one view to things that can never let us down!

If we see things with seeking eyes, on a search tone, scorching for things to happen then we will find that

"All the universe is setup for just one person—you" Much like a Paulo Coelho and Shahrukh khan mixture.

The man on the farthest of northern side standing; maybe has nothing to do with you but still if you see with those eyes; he is serving something to earth that is reaching us. Or if he is still doing nothing, then atleast he is contributing himself in the inter-minglation of this globe to be called as 'Earth'—where humans live."

She stopped speaking and I imprinted those words like anything.

Here, while I was preparing for my so near exams of social studies, the accumulation of all philosophies were getting faint.

All we were required to do was score marks and for once if we ever went blank on this exam day, we were to go almost blank with our futures as well. That humdrum of studies, rotting things up and drawing the best handwriting were the tools that we were settling our minds for.

In those two months of hostel schedule, 20 days already past, I was growing like the maid in our house being accustomed to the food and schedules of this place.

The sight of play in the mills playground similar to swami and friends seemed only like it was next possible in the heavens now.

Adolf sir's special kind of beating looked over now; it was special because he knew so perfect which chunk of the bumps generated the mightiest pain crossing the fortitude of human endurance.

That all looked over now. My friend and I went to history teacher's home to take some final day tips. She welcomed us well maybe because she was also leaving our school after exams would get over.

She gave her final farewell message to two of us, "Always be a good human being first"

God!!

Frankly, now I was rattled to the good philosophies that I was getting. Why so much of philosophies to me, why all strings of being sentimental chorded through me?

As if every human being who met me knew that I needed to improve.

I wasn't in a rehabilitation centre; I was still in my life. Though I had fallen but I would get up as well. What is the need to stare and perpetuate at me announcing as if; we're helping you buddy!

This was a moment when my self-being was getting shifted from that constant thought of past to a vision of doing something in future.

Yes, this was the moment, very similar to the laugh of Sisyphus, one of the characters by Albert Camus.

One Friday, I wore my white kurta pyjama and went for special prayers very patriotically to the mosque to make strong deals with God. After the prayers, while I was coming out in the jumbled mass of many, I intentionally tried to catch hand of the blind man who was just beside me to help him cross the road.

I got to say, that old man had lot of dignity and self-assurance than I could have thought on God. He threw my hand as I had tried to catch in a rude-concerning way.

I said to myself, "Idiot! I meant to help you"

He went on—small imbalanced steps, turning head right then left in an affirmed constant walk hurrying to get on the other side.

When he crossed the road, I thought to clarify him that I was just intending to help him to cross the road.

On the crossed road, he had a different soul awaiting to get installed; he came out of the rudeness covering and in the gentlest way escorted with a smile said, "I know that son. But what is the need to see me with pity, that the audacity of being blind just gets louder and further unbearable for me to handle.

You help me here and I seek help there. Why is the stare of discrimination so loudly peeping on me? I'm just a man without sight; that's it."

That old man though had a smile but wasn't less harsh in his words.

He went on to give his finishing words, "the inability to see something isn't the dividing factor in any of us."

He smiled as if I was witnessing the first smile on earth by a human being; it was so new. He may never have seen his smile in the mirror. Maybe he didn't know that in the same jumbled mass that he just crossed, there were some wanton desirous eyes wanting everything, maybe he didn't know that some eyes were beautiful with magical mascaras and plucked eyebrows, maybe he didn't know that some eyes had hopes and dreams and maybe he didn't know that some eyes were deep and mysterious as well.

How could he know anyway!!

A query to myself: what would have Adam thought when his eyes had felt heavy before he felt asleep for the first time on earth, the first sleep . . . what would have gone on his mind!!

Or for any other matter, the blood that was running in his body, the mind that he beheld, how different everything would have been for him.

With a subconscious mind and not so drastic changes, I was being introduced to a new situation of life where I was meeting examples who were ambassadors of the unusual change; turning the negativity into silver lining.

All this time, I had continued to react as if I was an ambassador to the sorrows. If even somebody talked good to me, I would dig up the matter deep and come out discovering a fruitless emotional part of it.

But, here I was in a sudden gust of change hailing me to be a part of happiness and suggesting the same thing ever—'See all around you; everybody is happy, why are you so sad?'

There are many times when we have no answer to a certain question and that is the time when we need to identify the demand of change associated with it and adapt it.

Why was I so sad? This was the question that I was asked by the whole world and I had no answer. An identifiable change was not seen yet but the element of 'need' to change was discovered which was half enough.

When God instilled the need to change on certain thing, he did not install a software like I did in computers and it started working instantly. There was no such tablet he had put in me called 'change' that would start its work as soon I realized it but we were needed to work towards the change.

We ate a lot in hostel especially at nights where we owed ourselves to study the whole night. That trying to study was the whole lovable buzz.

In those tension peak days, I was seriously missing the wrestling matches, the undertaker must have now beaten his long rival Brock Lesnar or Swami and his team mates must have received the full cricket kit; these things often came to my mind.

I liked concentrating on these things because yet I had lots of fear concentrating on atoms and molecules.

Studies for me basically was an invention by people to keep their children busy and schooling was quite the right method because in pursuit to keep their child's mind engaged, they also landed up filling up their mind with extra ordinary knowledge.

Apart from my world's philosophy, days of thoughtful strategies, exam day had finally come onto us. It was social studies—a cluster of geography, economics and history.

My country Nepal was smaller than its neighboring countries; that I had found through geography. History was interesting till some people; but I wasn't ready to learn from all of them. Economics was realistic but again I didn't like the deep down assumptions of the subject.

Nevertheless, it was the day I had to remember everything from what Jinnah did in the train to prove his innocency to the lady's allegation through his cigar from where Andaman and Nicobar was located to what made economics stand so important to study in our lives.

I jotted down everything on my mind and I don't know if ever asked again all questions, would I be able to tell or not, but this was that one day I had to jot down all in the best handwriting possible.

Our exams started on that tensed room, we were introduced to the invigilator for the examination and he instructed us to the proper filling ways of student's information before we were to start writing our exams.

Nobody had forgotten a single piece from the geometry box, equipped with bundles of extra pen, pencil and other stationary. The romantic couples who always flaunted besides each other in the classroom acted as they had never known the counterparts, such was the seriousness.

Once the seats were arranged, everybody checked their four sides—front, back, right, left and tried measuring the stature of help that might come in a difficult situation. The invigilator bored us with his line of advises—Take a deep breath, recall everything, think about your parents, think about your future and such things; nobody dared to yawn or gasp in philosophical wonders.

The constant rustle of papers, usage of scale and erasers were the only clattering sound that put the still picture of our examination hall into some movement. Asking of extra sheet for one bent all of us to compare and compete with the amount of writing.

Exam probably was easy because I also was able to do it without much hassles. We all left school with adulation of the given exam and preparatory readiness for the coming ones.

Our first public examination was over. We celebrated in the evening at hostel. The setting sun looked more blushing, dinner tasted more delicious, moon looked more expressive and sleep approached with most calm. My other two mates in the hostel were also happy because I had done well, that was good to see in their eyes.

Parents had yet not phoned me probably so that I am not disturbed. The milk in the morning was a slight reminder that we had four exams still left. I was easing out with the pressure.

Next was maths with 3 days of gap. I was revising the practice of all sums. It was the hardest subject for me but I came out well with this as well in the exam.

Then came science, 2nd language and English finally.

All examinations came with sheer excitement and fear but went out from our minds as we had never ever studied those subjects.

Board exams were over for us, I had unturned a milestone today. I still remember such happiness in all of my friend's faces as if they had screeched down to make things finally done. Everybody's face tiled up to dark circles and ingenuity to the hard work they had done.
My face, if I could just see my face to this day without the mirror; from somebody else's eye.
How happy must have I been on that day!

Boys as if pleading to all the outgoing people to scratch something with pen in their white shirts as the final farewell message, girls out-showing they had a handycam all their school life but that they just didn't show up because it was to be used only on this day. How happy were those faces!
Everybody looked ready to this day; beautiful girls were probably not to be seen again so frequently. Good friends still silent because we knew we would meet up again and again. It was the not-so-good friends that we were busy dealing first.

We met almost all teachers concerned; those who were shaggy, those who always attempted to be busy, those who were good, those who were too strict, those who were too loose on exams and those who were the best, we met them all.

We headed towards auditorium. As per school's culture, principal ought to speak something on the podium addressing us. She directly questioned tickling as if she was the world's finest wisdom-giver ever discovered, "how many of you have promised to meet again after you people get out of here?"

Everybody was gearing their murmuring sound like a child with smiles as if admitting their mistake—"Oh!" exalting with a flaming sound of 'hmm yes, I did'

She declared boldly, "the promise to be false because when you get out of here, it will be as if you are throwing a one lakh rupee of note in one end of the river and you hope that it will meet you at the other end."

By this example, she didn't outrightly reject our meeting idea but she only gave a less probability over the thing.

Everybody on that mind wondered and reacted—'wow, how honestly does she speaks!'

She continued, "Do not be sad today over you people's separation but be happy that you will miss some of your friends."

I wasn't so strongly tied up with too many friends but still I got the romanticism through her words at that time.

She was tickling and adjusting her glasses every now and then with her strong and definitive voice coming directly from the epiglottis with breakage in pronunciations resembling proper literate women.

Very quickly, she was nearing to conclusion, "Even a stopped clock is correct twice a day, but you people are an ongoing clock which is most certainly to be correct at every split second. And wonder if I stop you here at this point of life, would you be satisfied being correct two seconds in 24 hours?"

We echoed to our principal ma' m—A long Nooooooo with almost a kind of hypnotism to the effectiveness with which she was speaking.

We had to put lot of heavy usage of cranium to understand the enigma of a stopped clock example; our mind was in that phase.

"Being parted in this part of life is a happy necessity," were her final words thrown onto us.

I wished to hear more from her but that's the way I suppose things are. As per economics too, an orange's tasting satisfaction reduces if we ate more and more but the taste as the first one is incomparable.

Some boys had arranged the high speaker music system and everybody was called up to the stage for their last dance on the tune or putting it more aptly not on the tune but in anyway dance, just dance out with girls, boys— everybody being invited to grow wild for this moment as we were being parted away now.

I often stuck myself to many thoughts just on times when I shouldn't be thinking. This time too, I watched everybody from a good distance. Even the quietest of creature had the license today.

With songs being changed every now and then, the best of collection boys had accumulated all their precious time of exam, environment that had turned dim with the soft ambience, thence came time when I too was ready to flow with the music and the thought that 'this precious time'

Would I ever regret that I didn't thump up on the music with my friends when I was at this prime age. This time, I was being surrendered to be as the world was, as people were; I don't know good or bad.

Why so much of struggle, why can't I simply go and dance on the tune, what's the fuss on being thoughtful as such?

Every clicking of time said, "I am going. Bye!" Could it not stop for a second, atleast let me complete my understanding with the moment.

This was no fishing time to pervade with philosophies, I too went on the stage and danced in a corner with my best buddies.

Nobody shocked, nobody opposed yet some stares prompting 'see how simple was it!'

Everything was over.

My best friend's father came to take him in the car; I also got in for a one hour pleasing drive towards home.

What a sense of achievement was there in the car, "we had done it, man!!" were the only spoken words that I and my friend conveyed through eyes.

The intoxication wasn't there just in the alcohol, I was feeling beautiful with myself totally enthralled, ready to shout in the open air, ready to take on the world, ready to take on everything.

"How happy will my father be," I told my friend in the car.

Well before the evening I reached home, the food that served looked tidy on the table.

Dad wasn't home, mom's usual happiness could not have given the clue for how happy could have dad been. I eagerly waited for him to return from the factory.

Meanwhile, I and mom shared talks; about hostel, about leaving school, about bidding farewell. She was smiling but not in the full swing.

I was still eagerly waiting for dad. When I had failed and my father had gone to try if they could upgrade me somehow. That night my mom had confessed plainly that she had never seen dad being more disappointed than this day and he was nearly in tears. On being known about this, I was less saddened about my dropping-out in the grade than of knowing father's almost cry due to me.

All the time of my board exam, I had sub-consciously waited to find out, how happy would my dad and mom be when I will say to them, "today I have crossed the iron gate" The suffering that I had given to them in those dead moments of pride, could it ever be reconciled!

Mom's interpretation of watching heavens and realizing the achievement was a too far distance to handle. A distance of 50 year living life almost, how could I be living in that enigma and paradox of not achieving something here in this life, to achieve dad's happiness could just be a fine phase of achievement here in this earth.

The evening had sulkily dropped its presence to the trickling red light so beautifully immersed with the coating of everything on its way to wrap up with the days affair.

Dad came home late in the evening and though I had no barometer to measure how happy was dad; he looked well satisfied seeing me. We greeted each other and then the waiting for dad had diversified the eagerness of mine. He was nodding his head, speaking less.

Yet, we all sat and talked many more things until I went to a relaxing deep sleep in the silent unbathed universe.

To encounter both dad and mom's half smile was not so encouraging. I had gone out of home for the first time for over a month, something must have gone at home that has crippled both of them, or for atleast dad would have pinpointed every detail of 'how did exams go?'

I was eager to know what event has caught up when I was not here.

The next day I caught up the old accountant for whom privacy was an idiot's game; he was flawless to tell anything. He made me know that the mortgaged van was taken by the bank due to non-payment of the debts.

He said, "They came in one morning, asked for the keys and took it off"

It wasn't a matter about van getting disappeared but it was all about pride getting disappeared.

I carefully never asked about van to parents but within a week it was back again at the portico occupying its place.

My dad was in serious debts but I was more thoughtful about my own landing up in future.

Chapter-6

I had come down to the mid of 2003. Couple of days went on with my self-thoughts for further studies of 11th and 12th, I informed dad about my willingness to go Delhi and study. We tried initially in some good schools and when I was almost done with admission possibilities, I was pulled back and convinced to study in the same school and go out probably after completion of 12th due to family's not so good financial position at the time.

I had to settle lots of score with myself before I joined the same school for 10+2.

Life had shown the other track but just then it threw me back to the old track refusing to take me in.

Two years was a long time; a real difficult one for me to pass, but my dad had a convincing power very strong on me and his influence was like even if he told me to jump from a cliff assuring that nothing would happen when the fall is completed, I couldn't have given an extra thought on doing that.

My dad had told to me at this while that sometimes you perspire so much to achieve what your dream has always been that when you have almost achieved, it feels far less smaller than to how much you had mettled and perspired to achieve it.

IIis suggestion revolved around—Never have a small vision, there is no limitation on how much could we ask to God. He has got abundance and so always carry no less than a full bucket when you have got a chance to visit his infinite ocean.

I was basically being asked to cultivate a dream for myself from dad. But there was no dream whatsoever that I should have been cultivating.

Everyday I stepped into school bus sadly as if I was crippled down with stature.

In between those two years, major happening that approached was Faiza's marriage. My father had lots of preparation and mom's arrangement were as if going on from the time my sister was born.

It was a time when my moments with Faiza would all fade out. I was very happy for her and I remembered every talk from her, the critique of my favorite song 'mere samne wali khidki mein' to the acknowledgement of buying *chakus* for her.

On her marriage evening, I was willing to notify myself infront of her so that she remembers wonderful brother all her life. I ran to the market to buy a gift for her with very little money on my pocket. I wanted to meticulously seize this moment with the focus light on me and her like my favorite movie director. I was a confused soul; it was no new encounter but it was seriously hitting me at this time. After self-interpretations, I bought a handkerchief perfume which cost just 40 rupees and the only reason I could see it purchasing was because of its difference from ordinary gifts—'A handkerchief perfume, not any ordinary perfume'

I had carefully thought standing in the shop whether to purchase it or not and here, when I brought this gift so well wrapped up, she did not even care to have a second look for what her brother has brought. It was stacked and piled up into many other huge gifts by so many people, my gift was all lost in the shacks.

Emotions started flowing from my side and though I had presumed my sister to be special, she wasn't special at all. I had thought her to be special only because she was my sister.

She was also part of the same ordinary people who flowed with the world and who if read a great theory or philosophy by some famous author in a book, tended to follow those because it was said by such and such people.

Faiza was no special, my principal wasn't totally wrong when in a competition, she opined that her support won't be for any person just because he/she is from our school or from our country but I would only support if he/she is good in that particular field from others.

Time passes by, sun regularly goes down. Time comes up, the sun rises up again.

If ever I had to present a justification for my staying up at home after 10th to my far off gone friends, to whom I had talked so big and motivated as in equal I bullied them all those time and it was in a way 'my' presence and motivation that shook them to have that mind to reach where they had reached.

That justification could come on the line for the two marriages that went in my home. One of Faiza's and next as I was nearing to class 12th, my eldest brother—Sheezan.

My father in his life had conducted heart throbbing arrangements in the marriage of his brothers. But if impermanency was a permanent feature of life, that feature told him that he could not possibly do the same thing again for his son.

My eldest brother, whose marriage mom wanted so desperately because as a mom, she had yet not seen that phase and neither as a brother had I seen, how was it like having a brother's wife, what element did a new wedded wife brought in a man's life.

That desperation wasn't exactly to the fact—'we wanted it' but more appropriately the desperation was because of our inability in performing his wedding due to the financial let-downs.

Brother would as calmly wait with no signals by framing different kind of satirical sentences. Mom would quietly groom her wants in an unheard silence of preservation. Father would give his best efforts in work resembling only efforts can change, nothing else.

The fourth member was I; unable to do anything, analyzing as a perfectionist, pitying was the whole day's game.

Dad listened almost everyday after the morning prayers in the mosque; the recitation of Quran to the fact that 'we will be in struggle every now and then' why wasn't he less obscure to the hard times we were in.

When I failed, why didn't dad see me from that light of viewpoint, 'I was struggling' that's it . . . no big deal, no traumas, no hardships just a part of the game.

However
Dad's courage and mom's willingness tempted them to set the date of the wedding without any readiness to the things that would have come in terms of finances. Brother's silence was yet not broken.

Dad kicked here, dad kicked there, mom thought here, mom thought there but somehow the hardship were greater than the efforts.

I was enthralled to attend a debate competition where our school head boy stated 'Everything has two perspectives' but all these years, I found it so common in everybody's mouth in lieu of bringing the talk in a stalemate position that its heaviness was almost lost.

Our hardship may whatever had the perspective, it vowed to reach one thing—suffering.

Nobody in home knew that dad cried out of frustration in solitude at times and so it was enough for him to convey that 'Amen problems are now screeching more than the moment I thought your failing was the ultimate thing to see'

I felt relaxed on his conveyance of this thought but unrelaxed to the pitiness.

I still remember the dinner, yes I do remember.

We all four sat in the dining table with heavy thoughts on everybody's mind—how are we going to do it with just around 10 days on hand.

From where are we going to manage the finances; that ask looked crazy, very crazy!

That dinner as we started, nobody wanting to eat but everybody trying to show one another, "it's okay, we will do it!"

As per habit, I finished my dinner and washed my hand the quickest. Just then as I reached for the towel, mom threw those beautiful pinching words, "We've managed it!"

Some eyes went numb, brother's face stretched to a smile I don't know how much it could have been lengthened if there were no shackles in the jaws.

Mom as if breaking Da Vinci Code, we trusted in her words; 'we've managed it' could only refer to 'we've managed the finances'

We cared less to ask the pinpoint details but in that seized moment; we said to ourselves, "this is the smile that comes when you have trans-shifted from struggling phase to a struggled phase."

The pre-dinner phase and the post-dinner phase had a world's difference. Mom's oration was something like Brutus' speech to the mob perfectly entangling everybody to what they wanted to hear. Though her smile was sewn to a concern 'but there is else enough to do'

Father's unreported smile was visible to all of us.

As a child, I had gone to school with my brother in bicycle. How strong did he look from my eyes . . . with an ability to ride that two wheeled machine, so many friends flaunting aside him including girls, big classroom for him, big professors and sometimes he even talked English. It looked as if he knew all the mysteries of life.

As I grew, same features drawn, things looked very casual and now today was a time seeing a whole different set of features being conveyed by him: Pitiful young man, hair falling, forehead expanding and so three constant lines plastered signifying tension, lost to the simple techniques, incumbent and jumbled up to the inescapable strings.

It was long that I had not felt my inclusion among my family with equality but I too was included to the smiles that we constantly shared giving each other, glaring each other and embracing each other.

Father felt proud that his belief on 'somehow we'll manage it' hasn't gone unheard. I stood there watching faces of my small family. I could hire a philosopher all my life if he had different ways to express the moment.

We were tied-up for what to say!

She had asked from one known person, four lakh rupees as a credit; my father couldn't have done that and on any other occasion, that was unacceptable as well but for this moment everything looked okay.

How happy were those faces, we sat down like victor warriors, God smiling onto us and we saying, "yes, we trusted you!"

That was the finest dinner I ever had.

The wedding's core arrangement was finalized. The pursuit of creating that happy environment in a marriage had lots of cost and I was witnessing it so close.

I would earn someday surely, have best of things someday but I can't ever come back in this time of life and give my parents all the money they require for the wedding.

Small problems at my level were that cousins, family, friends would come from far places and the news of my failureness of being downgraded would get more and more publicly out.

Embarrassment was to be faced, my option of writing a letter and leaving everything came just in moments as such.

I wondered if somehow something can happen and I become unavailable for the marriage, though I would have lost so much of joyfulness, but my encountering with these humiliations were far more concerning matter to me.

Humans' fortitude in bearing pain created by God was too much. My Urdu teacher who had a skull cap endured on his head as a reputation appraiser to the profession that he was involved in. The resplendent black point on his forehead was a significant gift by God upon the reputation he had earned perfectly acclaiming his accountability as a *maulana* often embarked, "Human's caliber in bearing the pain had a limit."

I don't know if he understood that my limit in attending his classes were at pinnacle but he often reminded, "You could attend more"

It was his pinnacle ability of cleverness that he thought was very interesting for Amen but it wasn't, for sure.

When he grew serious and really interesting, he just took the talk to a bit higher level, he said, "sometimes its death that comes to a person with thanks for the reason that it has finally come.

Because, we often reach a stage of life where the caliber of attending the pain becomes unbearable and that's the moment when you thankfully accept death and embrace its coming. Invention of death-something that ceases everything; looks as the finest invention 'life' ever made for itself, the pain is taken away all at once."

I thought his notion could completely be called as 'over-spoken' but again I wasn't sure if death won't be embraced if it came at a peculiar stage as this man was facing. He probably said such things over the frustrations that he himself was in. About a month back, his son in law had expired due to the fall of a sky lightening, daughter had almost cracked down and their childrens had hard time upbringing. He was still bearing all that alive here at this far off place to earn a meager sum of money. Certainly bearing pain had a high limit.

The wedding date clicked, guests came, brothers arrived and frantically almost everybody knew that I was downgraded. To some people whom I didn't ever wanted to know this secret of mine knew the details so clear.

If I happened to visit Sudan or any other of the poorest country and tell people that the biggest tension in my mind is the failureness that I had seen while I was at such and such class. The struggle of these people were so hard for food that it wouldn't have been a surprising factor if they killed me instantly.

Yes, people had far bigger and genuine blocks of tension.

When I crossed the mills ground, all the boys knew that this boy once was a throbbing piece for the ground who actually set the trend of many things that we are doing today.

I would often stand their, dumbly thinking on too many things, but no one invited me back again though the boys had changed.

Khurram had diligently settled with father's tailoring, Tarzan had shared his wish of working in google company when he grows up but he eventually had settled down with a goggles store. Tariq had immersed himself into studies, Yasar and Rafey had gone to different place.

After being left out from my actual class and mills boys; I did not have very much courage to make friends altogether again.

So, I was everywhere but in actual nowhere more soundly.

One day when I mumbled my wallet from most inside pocket to the publicized view, I found a letter—crumbled, jumbled, wrinkled. The whole surrounding gazed at surprise, echoing, 'For how long have you been hiding your emotions?'

This letter I had written for Faiza to give her on the wedding day. But the feelings had gone so disoriented that giving any kind of written stuff entailing everything in those two pages wasn't worthwhile.

They had no charm, they had no mystiques or heaviness. They were just two pages of filled matter.

The letter read as-

"Dearest Sister,

On this commencing last letter, I borrow no one to write uncaring of the bad handwriting I possess, not unmindful of the moments we have shared from our childhood, you being critique of the songs I sung and the cricket I played . . ."

I read this much and couldn't read more

Those were idiot emotions, nobody cares. I was only following a trend, the Hollywood one, where any hero from any war writes beautiful emotional lines in such a stylish way.

Faiza might get thrilled that I wrote her something and next thing she looks is grammatical errors. She may never reach the point.

Chapter-7

*T*hose two years passed by, it wasn't quick. It was very long. It was tough to everyday string out with those unethical bumming boys who supposed themselves cool with guitars on hand.

I wasn't one of them. Time has passed anyway. I did give my class 12th examination well and fine. Everything went good. I had yet again signed in the boys shirt and got myself captured in the digital camera of girls.

The hard time was spent. I had stayed in the same paying guest cum hostel just the accompanying boys had changed. The moonlight shone spectacular when I grew happy.

I itched myself; why am I not all the time same?

It is this intangible thing: 'happiness' that we all do so many activities for or to put it more appropriately; it is this intangible thing that people look to achieve at the end of the course. A country expenses so much of amount on sports when there is other inevitable expending that a country needs to make; it is for that intangible honor and pride that a country puts so much of effort in.

Similarly, it is that happiness; that simple happiness for which a man perspires all his life.

Whenever I saw autobiographies of legends in history channel, they spoke things as if they were the kings of time. It looked so influential; Andre Agassi on my days of gap after exams highlighted one statement so profoundly; "Either you do things differently or don't do it"

I had talked very big infront of anybody to whom I got frank with; they saw me with a toiled eye, not able to make a correct assumption—this boy 'can he be something?'

Then, with activities of my own, I was slowly but definitely dropping the baton every now and then, the baton that was being passed down by the leaders of the past; by the visionaries of past.

It was fearsome to think: what after 12th?

This question's answer wasn't the answer of only this ask but also a referral to how my future was going to be shaped or what sort of ambitions could I possibly catch up to become.

The suffering and the artist who creates aren't the same.

God truly had his playful mind activated when he was dictating the policies to be implemented that were to run here on this land.

Everybody was so peaked up with tensions for how their future was to be carved out; in what direction.

I remember my cousins being so much tensed about cleaning rooms and praying namaz while they were at home and when they had no work to do at all but no pennies trepidation while out for useless fun and enjoyment.

So from a sullen mind, it all looked as if humans had made those tensions, whimsical dreams, future humdrums, almost everything just to keep themselves busy and to get enjoined in the busy-ness of the world.

I mean what's a worth not going out anywhere, not doing any work, not having visions of doing anything just to the sake that one had to pray at five different odd times a day, what's the worth!!

On the contrary, namaz for Muslim's most intense purpose itself is to be busy with the world and on the same time do this five minute activity signifying that however busy may I have got, whatever the sadness is, however the happiness is, I am not so enjoined in the rejoice or to the sadness that I've forgotten 'you'. That's it!

Well, if I had to evaluate myself with things in a broader perspective, I had not just failed in studies but I was continuously failing in all the fields that I was entering due to a well pretexted background and the only one losing due to me was me.

With one event of yourself losing, we ought to stand up again and say; ok next time, I'll try not to succumb in this small ground. But, I have been so lost with that one event that I am further derogating and derogating myself with no hint of uprising.

That one event of failureness has caught my tail and has created a kind of chain relaying the effect in whatever field I am entering.

No, this could not go on, if I am to hold the fate myself, I have to hold it then—very, very strongly

Past had clearly shown, what my achievements had been in my view were mere laughs for the satirical human walkers.

My achievement was that I had walked everyday two kilometers from school to home and home to school to save that heavy two rupees at a time when I should have been lurking in the thumps of childishness studying in ninth grade.

My achievement was that I had hardly purchased new clothes at a time when as a growing youth, I should have got the romanticism of 'this precious time'

My achievement was that I had left a fantastic beautiful liked girl due to failing with whom I could have gone to think my life in a stage.

My achievement was that I had foiled myself in the troubles of my parents as fresh and as lively to the problems as they were at a time when I should have been a freefall in nature with anything done pretexted in the grounds of 'he is only a child'

My achievement was that I had stuck to my principles so strongly at a time when I should have been flexible as an immature mind.

I had failed in grades.

Now, how big is that failureness to shadow down whatever little intangible I have achieved?

When I had passed the iron gate, I had my first feat achieved. Now why is everybody adamant to make me know of the fact that it's nothing, there are more harder hurdles to face. Why! Is it because I am superiorising myself that I have crossed it, is it?

My questions had no answers because, I was surrounded by no one. I was wandering in an immense sea of loneliness.
My sister's presence was with me but her absence was too.

What was an achievement afterall, who decided the quotients of an achievement?
If my heart was satisfied and somebody was happy with me, could it not be concluded as an accomplishment, a triumph?

After my 12th had finished, my far-gone off friends now guzzled to whichever place they were, I had no spaces of justification left to present them.
The chords of excuse can only be maintained until a time it doesn't upbeats the pincers of fakeness.

What after 12th?
One of my closest cousin Adnan had asked me to cultivate a dream, he should have better told me a dream too.
When I saw the hoarding boards at the most staked up places of the Indian Cricket Team, I had to divulge myself in thoughts or else my blood was water according to Rang de Basanti.

It needed a big shot. A shot to clear off the debts that my dad had taken when he had pursuit of establishing everything again.

How tough was this lofty game there, in that part of country. What it took for a man to reach that level of stature.

The idea was so vague, I feared if anyone would consider it as a dream that I was vying towards. Afterall, from millions they needed just 11. That 11 who represented a nation, that 11 who overturn the price of pride.

Some sort of disagreement would have dad thought that I was going through with the working condition of mind if I had exposed him that I was in such thoughts or such was a dream that I was cultivating.

Dad's caliber had profounded him to suggest me to take a bucket whenever you get a chance to visit the oceans of the giveness of God. But does the feasibility of askness bleaker if I decide to take something more convenient and sophisticated than just a bucket.

The idea was too big. Smile as an immediate reaction to the idea was no less horrific and heart wrenching.

Yes, sitting in this country called Nepal, I was thinking to play for the Indian Cricket Team.

As big the idea sounded the same length did fear rested its arms. Often philosophies that people gave were one sided and even if we wanted their is no other or flip side of the story.

If Adnan had showed me a philosophy to focus on a certain thing that we eye to achieve then the flip side conquered to ask 'what if you don't'

That flip side is very very dangerous looking view. What if I don't reach that ambition.

Well, for a man to do something, he has to first of all replicate the authenticity of his attainment.

What would have apes thought when their senses were broadening or what would have people thought when the landscapes were not discovered.

They would have thought the world ended where their eyes stopped visioning. But, somebody went on and said, 'no buddies we have a world forward too!'

If nobody had thought what I was thinking and nobody had achieved what I might achieve; could not be the reason why I shouldn't have achieved.

It would have been better if I could have hunged up to an immature childish state. Here, at this adultery state, every atom were too much jumbled up.

My brother who had stayed up in Delhi for so long was my thickest block of hope to get admission through in Delhi University, this was kind of an initiation when my-made principles as a child were being shaken up, when I was taking help of people, in an unethical mode.

My thoughts were sparkling clear to everybody—Amen was to land up in Delhi next.

Studies hadn't occupied the chunky part in my living ever but it was an integral part which mattered so much to my relatives, to the call 'my son is a degree holder', to my friends who would ask all this next 3-4 years 'buddy how is your studies going on?'

One thing that I was passionate commencing to the fact that I wanted to go the capital of India was to check my standards in all aspects that I wished to do something in.

If cricket was passion, India was home.

I waited for so many days until my results were out. It was such a captivating morning. The time was 7 o'clock. I caught up a friend and reached a cyber café door before 6.30.

We waited catching up with other friends in cell phone if anybody got any news but we feared to the awaitness. I wanted not to listen any kind of updates.

Results were out and I had yet not gone into the notion of whether I will pass or not, but it was the humdrum of percentage scoring. Results were out.

I was in the first division lot. But the term 'in millions' itself was so disgracefully presented by my uncle and a satire to non-thankfulness which was preached to me by my relatives. It brought to a notion that whatever you do, already someone has done better than that.

It was an achievement for me to have passed class 12th. It might be a very normal picture to life for others but it wasn't easy for me. When my dad explained to me the logic of thanking God when we sneezed, he constantly reminded of what's easy for you can be startling difficult for another.

It might have been normal and smooth functioning towards the upgrading process in stages of schooling for many. For me it was a task hard and painful at my price.

The exemption from everyday wearing that white uniform was pleasing, no monotonous routine of catching the bus at 6.30 in the morning was a privilege, getting away with the rotten learnings for a day in pursuit of scoring maximum was an escape, grooming everyday in the best way possible to the thought 'what would girls think' was an exception.

Though not being able to see Nikita as frequent again was little distasteful.

There was a change in the pleasures of routine. The mounted shape of 'rocked rice' which I liked calling, with lots of *dal* flowing in little streams; that had the 'taste' which I ate around 4 in the peak of tiredness and to the fulfillment of empty stomach that I had carried the whole day with all sorts of activities in the school premises was lost.

An expression of coming down in stature at school with a display of sullen face explicating 'I am meant for far better stuffs than these' had a different charm of patronizing in everybody's view. A pat of calmness drawn in my own soul of 'how busy and sacrificing you are' was less audible. The unnecessary arguments with teachers and faculties on not-so-important topics now deemed less so frequent. This was all the part of the change in routine or a psychological transformation into a more open and challenging world coming out from the easy cushion of everyday going to school in the school bus and coming back the same way occupying the whole busy-ness of mind.

I had all the time in the world to do almost anything. I was the king!

When I reached home at four during the time of school, I hurriedly ate my food as a routine and ran for cricket practices but with all the time in the world, I had grown lazy to go in no hurry and with ease at the proper time of around three for the practices. Basically; I was so immersed with the tight schedule that was set for myself that I wasn't liking the breakage and casualness offered by time.

For so many years from childhood, I was a part of those schooling schedule hours, but not now.

With passage of class 12th, to answer the question of 'what now' pitched evenly more responsible.

Being confused was a result of the playful policies that God had designed for us. He on his part wasn't wrong as well. Bad times kept us alive and so it was necessary in our lives, I supposed so.

I knew God could be very ruthless at times. He could order the soul-picker to kill all the family and might leave just the day born baby alive.

Had somebody gone to ask the parents of that child over to the question, "Can I take your soul?"

Could any one of us have said, "Ok?"

Now it was serious time.

On those days, my brother Ezel who had come from Delhi completing his bachelors was the first one to have been asked this question, "Ok, So what have you planned to do in future?"

The question wasn't out from the blocks of bombshell amazement, but it was as normally asked by dad as it could have been for the dinner. I held my ears vast open to the conversation they were having from the other room. Someday I shall be independent as well, my dad was in desperate need of help majorly in finances.

The awaitness before applying in colleges for further studies had stipulated lots of time to gather lots of options. With an immature child, if I was exposed to lots of options to pursue my career on, then coming to this state of adulthood those foolish options had yet not left my hand.

And seriously, too much of options is only a medium of confusion.

I was too much interested in journalism but then I had to do some real hardcore business as well because I supposed myself too good in the tradings and all, but then again my finest dream for the Indian cricket team could not be overshadowed.

Now, here I stood back again catching the plated strings of confusion like I was standing back again in the stockpile of hanging clothes in a clothing store with so much that I could buy yet not being able to buy.

On those days, it was so very necessary for me to have that rope of determination clutched hard.

If I listened to odd people who had never reached to the pinnacle of success just because they had never thought that they could reach to those starry level could not all come in a round off reason for why I couldn't reach somewhere their around.

I knew this trait of many people who had an art of presenting an undone thing as a showcase of sacrifice burnt.

I couldn't follow this trait because then all my life, I would have thought only of this thing that I could have done at that part of life. My father's word, "that of being unable to do something is one of the worst things" would just be a 'fuel adder' in my living forever.

I knew people apprehended sacrifices made by human beings but why always!

Sometimes, a man merely sacrifices for the sake that he can make a sonorous speech all his life and replace his inability to the face of sacrifice.

Cricket and to reach that level of the game was no less as that star.

The underlying problem was that I could not just give my life a risk and leave up everything to get in the team which had a crucified requirement of 11 out of millions.

The path could only come up with studying in India and playing cricket the same time, so that the lone risk doesn't screech out loud.

Journalism was at its peaked askance on my mind. This was the time when I had all the right to file a complaint against the policies designed by God. Why such a short spanned time?

If Influence was liquid, I was the ocean.

My language teacher in Nepali taught the best poems and stories I could ever recount. One of the poems described, "One viewpoint says, this small life, what can we do.

And the other view point confers; this big life, how much to do."

I dialogued myself often, "Journalism needs me desperately" I laughed at this tone of dialogue delivery as if I was a savior and an unprecedented talent entering in the media world.

There were far better men and women already involved in the business.

Well this was a phase of time, when I had to get upon the entrustment of dad that 'my son can do it'

How simple was it to do for many. But work was a far off thing, only the entrustment filling was so hard.

Finally it was admission time everywhere. Dad armed me well to send Delhi with good enough amount of money and mom equipped and kitted me fine to get prepared with anything from her department with well pressed clothes, toothbrush, oil, etc.

I was travelling alone to get to my brother-Ezel who like a magician would have taken me to college that I would point out and get me admitted there in the best manner; that was a poor deceptive piece of defense from me.

When I reached Delhi late at night for the first time, I was no less enthralled than as to my best moments.

Brother received me in his green tee shirt and I was witnessing the best things that India had manufactured because it had a simple banner—Capital of India. As I got inside his friend's car with an unclean view in dark night, I was almost assuming everything as some great landmark, this was the impression of this place to me. I yelled to myself in the backseat with so much of enthusiasm, able to do anything, "Now, I'm on!"

We chased up from the very next morning in Delhi University colleges but as if only the toppers had the right to come and enjoin with the admission procedures and saying 65% to the gate-keepers tended them to offer an all-together a different look. Was all of India scoring above than average? Boy belonging from an inferior county, Nepal had no right to thump up with the music as all others had done?

The view was skeptical. Running was worthless. Chilling was irresponsible. Waiting was idiotic. Laughing was insane. Crying was loss 'exposed' and returning was the only option.

It all looked impossible and probability only knocked in the face if I took admission in some private college. The hefty fee amounts, I could not burden my father once again.

I was so hopeless with the admission that I was happy to watch television and eat the home delivered food. A console gift is given to the last runner, I was also being given new pair of clothes alongwith a new mobile phone.

After the consoling, most probably in a well behaved way, I would be kicked out of Delhi and probably give a more secluding try in some other place.

When I talked to dad on phone giving him a hint of 'I am still trying' was emotional from me trying to deceive both the souls on either side of the telephonic talk.

I saw very beautiful girls there in the big malls, small floor of life in contracted homes and independent lives in the faces of women driving cars.

I had nearly stayed about 15 days unrealizing to the precious time of admission that was getting lost. I wasn't ready to counter the questionnaire of 'what's next'

I was nervous, I was heated and I was deceived.

Whoever had known me, knew very well that he has got all sorts of talent. I was less unambiguous to anything but it could have been very good if God gave me a personal meeting for some hours; I had important things to discuss with him. I had to exchange my soul in other body and see how did other people differ at situations. Basically, I had to see my standard.

Obvious laugh has to be plated in the faces of many, on hearing the idea of meeting with God. But if I was unambiguous then I was carrying credence as well. I could go on believing that I can meet God and that he will give me an appointment rather being obscure and terming it a 'fictional' thought.

People had gone beyond thoughts of script that people had set and that was the only thing that had set them apart from the normalcy.

If I had decided to choose Journalism and if I could grab all the etiquette that was needful in writing an article or a story than why was the fuss of a degree needed.

If business' only philosophy was 'grasping of opportunity' then what was a concerning matter in holding a graduate unused degree.

Then again what suited me was not suitable for everybody else in the world, neither I suggested all others to be as me. If one person is good, it isn't necessary the other one is bad. Ascribing antonyms in all matters wasn't needful as well.

With hippie smiling face and cool attitude expressing 'Don't worry Ezel, I'll manage something somehow' I was again moving back to Biratnagar with heartening thoughts and unlived victory once again failing to be successful in this small thing yet again.

How was my father then to get the belief 'Yes, my son can do it'

I got in the returning train very happy so that the sadness doesn't gets exposed infront of Ezel.

People in the world had beheld so big traumas with smiling faces reacting as an alchemist; knowing all the mysteries of living.

This period of life was very fearsome. I didn't know what I had to do nor did I know how to do!

When I reached back to Biratnagar, I with less excitement again perspired to see dad and his reaction as to 'Was he still expressionless from his part on my failureness?'

Or was all anger in accumulation ready to burst at me?

An assumption perceived that those who spoke less valued more. With the value addition, also adds is the mysterious element. My father had yet not burst into me even once over my failing in the grades and failing in so many minute things. His calmness, his showcase of encouragement 'I know you will do it' was heaved on me screeching down with all his voice of a pressure bestowing upon me. It would have been so better had dad clearly spelt out his fury, his anger, his frustration of confession 'the reality is that my son hasn't done anything remarkable yet'

But dad had remained quite all these years perplexing me to one fury that would outburst in what part, in what scenario.

Reaching back to Biratnagar, the center question was 'what, how, where to study?' I was more mingled up to everybody's reaction, my own hopeless thoughts.

In the intermission time while I was at home dealing with my own business, one morning I woke up to the news of death in our *mohalla*. An honest applauder of our game in the mills ground after the namaz, elderly man quite very same as to the age of my father, a laughing stock in the crowd especially when he described his wrong assumptions of a heart attack almost every night that he thought he had countered.

Today, he was dead with the same choke of not so good flow-ups with the heart about which almost every person had went on laughing.

I saw his face pale, dull and blackened. It was as if his dead body was a presentation to the non-believers as a justification that he really had problems with his heart. Encountering death scenes were a live showcase of strong realizations and uncommitted resolutions.

During the cremation, dad's freelance comment to one of his mates, "saaman *sau saal ki, pal ki khabar nahi*" was worth saying looking at the under-construction house of the dead man.

An expression flew from people of his own age so frightening and astute. Witnessing dead body was like an awakener to the notice, "Get prepared"

The site of janaza in the burial ground especially in the evening looked everybody's ultimate home; when we left this man quiet and calm in the slime, no complaints, no expressions, accepting the longer version of sleep. I think on these moments almost everyone promises himself to be good, never do a single wrong thing again because one realizes that 'really one is simply left alone in the questionnaire of God'

Father felt uneasy till 12 noon on the next day but I was busy thinking over my things.

It wasn't a suitable thing to talk when dad was busy thinking on himself so deeply feeling uneasy.

But frankly, I cared more up to my own business.

The time demanded to make strong decisions. Being loose now meant being lost all the while.

I had so many dreams, I could not have clutched by the family ties and sentimental strings.

The time demanded to make very strong decisions.

All I wanted to know was; what is in dad's mind?

Meanwhile, eldest brother Sheezan was blessed with a daughter. It wasn't a wholesome surprise because God had stipulated that 9 months so apprehensively. But a little plus and minus to the date was so good to have been waiting till the daughter popped out.

We had shared the same room for so many years until I led him to his own room on his first wedding night, he was the perfect face of jubilancy. From that day onwards of maintaining strict privacy with Sheezan to this day, seeing him so happy with his own daughter coming out of the labor room. What was that happiness afterall of owning a child? What was so special about having a daughter?

I could not have expected Sheezan to be happier, he was glancing and dancing with this new member of our honored family, murmuring in no-language which is assumed to be child's language.

Yet, I was more caring to my own business.

I waited for so many days until dad felt ease out of a mate expiring from the blocks of his own era, family adapting the entry of a new member. I was with everybody: with dad's uneasiness, Sheezan's happiness but then I was nowhere.

I had always been very strong. I had sometimes shown that things were a little too easy to do but while performing I had failed. I had sometimes stood in the setting sun and sought a fight with it to the notion 'you can't take the day away from me till I turn things right' I had sometimes taken water into a quarrel 'why don't you purify me all over once again from the marks of being left-out?' I had sometimes questioned the ability of trees 'why don't these wigs shade my matters of embarrassment'

Dad only hadn't been uneasy with mates being lost of his age and to an open secrecy that his time was nearing too.
Dad's right hand was an accountant who was same as to his age. Looking at the features, they might have gone to be the best friends had they not been divided in the strata of master and employee. To have been talking with the old unleashing accountant was uneasy. He revealed too many things going on in the business section, often prompting me to come out of the stony career thoughts and think about this old man—my father.

When the old accountant revealed about poor health of the business, it was serious time to do something. It dinted the impression of the correctness that dad had been portraying through his sullen reaction adapted all this time. Could have he been less thoughtful to think about his son but all these years he was bound to the limited resolutions he could make due to the loans, the hefty loans.

When the flawless accountant opened the no secret, he propelled in me the desire and passion to walk on a road to make atleast dad see that 'my son is walking alongwith' which should be half enough for him to get the power to fight in all kind of situations.

The accountant as a loyal employee had a sheer purpose to accommodate me with those attributes but I was more caught up to my own career making that could only come through more and more study in some different far off place.

To be thinking so much on these matters was possibly an outcome that dad had never asked for sympathy in any kind of direct or indirect manner. He was as quiet to problems marking 'only his own' as Sheezan was quiet yet desperate for marriage.

He only needed a little hope, he only needed a little courage and I believe he had all; because he always pronounced strongly, "If you have power to patience, you have power to win.

Win probably might not be in a direct view but with consolidation, with conviction and with satisfaction."

That is what dad taught me all these years but the patience that he beheld was only he beheld. It wasn't a portraying patience to everybody tending others to question, "what has he earned after all these years?"

The question's mouthpiece often would not be very far coming most of the times from mom herself surrendering the fortitude of endurance to adversity.

If I had embarked for very long in my childhood years though in whimsical thoughts—assumingly dad to be

God playing all things in the world, everything setup for me. Then it was because he had some statured thinking position of that rank.

Like cranium's capability wasn't the dividing factor to judge the humanity, the same way money wasn't the dividing factor to stipulate status of a human though the new world had ordered the philosophy in the opposite direction.

My mom had not seen so much of a poor life coming from a barrister father to an honored well to do family of my father. Dad's philosophy often also counted in the difference of the struggling and struggled phase.

"It was a world's difference," he emphatically pronounced.

My mother was an all-time namaz adherent and an aspiring woman to perform the hajj. I wasn't too much surprised to listen mom advising Ezel after the completion of his bachelors that "working everytime in wholesome correctness might provide you with very less chances of being rich"

She was like caught up in the tunnel named 'struggling phase' and when she would come out at the other side of the tunnel 'the struggled end' an all-together different human might get found out.

The loans were a burden in the shoulders of my father. He could not go on performing hajj with this burden nor was it appropriate.

The accountant made a thrilling revelation.

When I was 50 kilometers away from home giving my class 12th examinations catching the strings of emotions on 'dad doesn't even cares to phone me' the very same time dad was in a crucifying problem of his life. The factory was shut down by the bank authorities. It was sealed. A handsome nominee was to get presented to the butchers who had eyed on this piece for so long through auctions. The accountant knew the punch of his last sentence—"the factory was sealed"

I tried to recall the eye of my father who always walked in a 15 meter distance up to down inside home, hands clutched back, mouths shut, with intensified thinking. Those eyes were still numb, with no signs of help needed, no sympathies sought.

The factory was his lifetime payment. He was jobless for four years until he saw his first place to work. Then, he had to abruptly leave everything in separation and start back again from dust. He was pathetically helpless until he got to revise everything with the loan sanction. That was a good time because it was believed that loans would be paid back.

He very well was aware to what he had mounted up. From dad, I learnt apprehensively that if you send a man all naked outside in the midst of new faces, new people, new country then also that man has got a capability that he can earn a cloth, food and somewhere to sleep. That's a capability in-built in humans by God.

It was long back I had stopped taking money from my father's pocket. But I was still taking money from him, though not on the while he was asleep but while he was awake. It had a very little difference.

Suddenly in this part of life, I was getting exposed to this new attachment—my father.

This old man had done marvelous things though Sheezan had problems with dad introducing all of us to a phenomenon called loans even before we were born but my viewpoint said to slap him whenever he spoke thus.

It was very hard for me to wonder, how would have dad been, had he not been enrolled to the loan amounts. He was deeply accustomed and rooted to face problems in everyday living very similar to Sisyphus that he had mastered in it.

It was itching for new people like me to leave the phone ringing. For him to pick up the phone of the lender did not mean just to articulate but give reasons, find a new fakeness, laugh in the same tone, forget about God, forget about the next day that would come and his relishing in the fakeness would dimmer.

The phone sounded not louder but not even bleaker than to the call of my name in the morning assembly as the fee defaulter. There was it, that I learned the meaning of 'solitude' At first I was enthralled to have been tagged as the solitude fee defaulter and later I was panicked and disappearance with absence was the only rescue from all the eye-holders finding me when principle changed her role to a money collector standing in the podium.

I had missed many occasions of our school due to improper dress fondly advocating as 'I know what occasions I should be present in'

He was made for this tension. Had life been very easy for him, it would have also been pathetic for him.

When he was four and he lost his father, he wasn't a kid. When he was nine and his mother shouted on him to earn, he wasn't a boy. When he was 12 and made the first block of wall in the house, he wasn't a guardian. When he was 16 and took the first puffs of cigarette inside the toilet, he wasn't a grown-up. When he was 20 and took upon all the family, made his own industry, he wasn't an adult and when he was married at 23, he wasn't an oldie.

This was his story lived and my history learnt. He was a bad inspiration but a beautiful aspiration.

He was a bad inspiration because he had lived his life, he had done his duties and far better than that, he had made everybody live like a prince but if I ever tried to get in the same shoes then I might or might not succeed as the same and so he was a beautiful aspiration.

Accountant had done the trick. My next no-fictional hero was dad. Far better than Spiderman who was ready to fantasize me but unready to get me fantasized.

So what was the way I could help dad?

I knew the gravity of problem when they needed money for Sheezan'smarriage, I was a pitiful watcher then.

I had seen dad crying locked inside a room, I could curse myself so badly but I was a pitiful watcher back then as well.

If those were times when I couldn't tap myself as a savior or even helper, then I was doubtful if I could do something now.

So, better was it to be stone again and think about my career.

In fact, these days of waiting were good days. Though I had that sullen reaction plastered on the face but then deep down I was very secured.

On a slim night, I talked to dad after the dinner about my further studying.

For him, some guardian has to be for a child.

Suddenly, on the next chapters of life, I was landing up in Kathmandu, the capital of Nepal with a cousin residing there.

Dad knew very well that I wanted to go out of home and be a little independent but was distrustful on my individuality that he decided to make me stay under the guardianship of my cousin Adnan.

Adnan was an admirable man who was chasing his dreams at a very high price keeping in stake the cherishing youth of his, when and where he should had been lurking down in the making of mega bucks, brandishing golden youth.

It was very much for this man Adnan that I got ready for Kathmandu.

I was fearing if dad might convince me again to be in this place and study but he was a soul very much like me and so he sent me to the capital of my country. I hurriedly ran to Kathmandu for what if I miss the last entrances for getting in the finest management colleges of this place.

I was sent through air; this made the Kathmandu going more acceptable. This place was atleast a known place in the world. When I entered the chat room in the internet, people were not amazed as to where this place was.

The problem at small place is that whatever we do, it is rounded off in the spheres of being small but in big place whatever we do, small or big—it looks worthy and a thing to talk about.

Kathmandu had its own striking features. When I first visited the college, building stood tall and handsome, people looked friendlier, girls looked prettier, and the whole environment looked engaging. Now I had to get lost in all of this.

As the slim night ended, I was still in my bed with no flight stepped in, no college visited and no entrances given. It was all in a blissful dream.

I was okay to it because it showed that God was in little concerns with these matters.

Dad had gone weary with all the dealings that he had been doing all his time. For one strong reason, I hated Sheezan, Adnan who were grown and strolled in the new ordered world meaning 'strict business' having learnt all the managerial and business skills as per their assumptions in unreal and unlived situations.

Moreover, it was not even strict business mindset but it was their attempt in pursuit to sound like a literate and well understood featuring man by showcasing skills. It was their pathetic effort to show 'Had I done things in the place of dad, I would have done it all in a different and a better way indeed'

These two idiots were very similar to my mindset in schooling days where I used to think the whole day about how to cheat and pass the exam, all the new probable ways of doing it. They were no outlandish than this mindset because with everytime shouting at dad for 'how he did wasn't the way it should have been done' they produced and

manufactured a statement so well built-up that ever they failed, they would always have a backed-up statement 'My failing today is all the root problem from how dad did it'
They had in a way backed-up to the failureness that they would meet; they had perpetuated to the cunning mind.

Often they questioned dad over matters of how small worth was industry's name or what did he do else than mounting loans and many other questions for which dad had never been alert because he himself was the creator and maker with the only supervision of God.
He had never prepared statements for giving justification to anybody because he was the master of whatever he had done, good or bad.

What these two always missed out to think was that their askance were basically a question over dad's whole lifetime tenure in what he had done. He was a pitiful man.
I had seen his photograph wild in youth but had grown deplorable in his ageing.
He was king at a time when in the typical outset of Hindi movies, it showcased Kader khan, Amjad Khan and other villain real friends but as soon as one got lottery over money, Kader killed one villain scrutinizing and mangling the other villain to be the killer in collaboration with Amjad Khan with perfect picturization of stabbed knife in the hands of the 'proven' killer. And that Kader khan gets a young Prem Chopra as his son acting as the within age villain for Amitabh Bachhan. That was my father's time of kingship but not now.

My next no fictional hero was in trouble.

I went to the factory with dad to see how were things going on with the leather manufacturing. We went in our little van to cover the distance of 15 kilometers.

With too much of noise in the core operational area due to machines inside the factory, I realized there are some moments in time where we are totally ready to say anything, the most locked up matters of our heart.

Dad probably had many, many things but there was no one listening to him. His feeling of guilt and for me probably he thought 'what can he do' so my worthlessness always fused in to say him nothing.

In his very bright office in the day broad light where sunlight equipped the whole room as if it was paying rent to us, we sat and dad asked me, "Are you hungry?"

I said 'No,' half-heartedly. I was not the one to show 'I am sensitive' and reaching only to the mid-day, I am perished and broken to hunger.

Father asked me to call Majid.

I signaled the gatekeeper through movement of fingers to call him in patronizing under the banner of 'I am the youngest son of your employee.' I ordered him in a heavier voice to find Majid and send him in as if Majid was a running criminal and gatekeeper was the investigating officer.

"Old Majid must be with some village girls," dad joked.

Majid came in, "Go and bring samosas and cold drink for Amen," dad ordered this time.

I retired on the sofa, sat in half sleeping position acting as am so tired.

Dad asked, "Are you bored son?"

I said, "No" in small voice to retain the notion 'Yes I am'.

When he was free and in the mood, he talked brilliant things. He started, "Samosas of this small place is very good, something that you will miss all the while."

I sat quiet for a while, he sat quiet but he cared to break the silences.

He said, "You know one of our messengers before Muhammad had once been put into a shameful allegation with a girl. He was alleged, cried for many days and complained to God as he was the prophet.

He was soon out of the fake allegations but he was a furious prophet. God empowered him with the control of land obeying anything he could do with his help.

The prophet ordered the land to take that woman inside the land, deeper, ever deeper. Women was in world's amazement and wept for her life with whatever apologies she could present and forgiveness she asked continuously but then he ordered the land to completely digest her inside forever.

He was well satisfied with his act."

Dad broke the story for a second. "It was all part of the fate," It wasn't required from dad but he chose to mark the story this way.

Then he continued with the plot. "As that messenger was very happy over his doing; God told him that, Oh prophet! You were in anger and bursting with fury but had I been in your place, I would have forgiven her life upon one call of forgiveness."

That is what God told him, the story ended.

He had never talked relating to Hadiths and such maturely thought provoking story to me though I had become matured in all these time of emptiness. I wondered why he told me this incident from the history vault. Before Dad went out of the room; he told me one thing that I cant forget ever.

"There is one group of person with whom remains GOD. It isn't the people who pray religiously or lives a secluded meditation living.

It is the people who remain patient"

I thought Dad was a little wayward with this statement but he confirmed to me with the sentence from Quran "Inallaha Mu-a-ssaberin" meaning God is with them who remain patient.

He let me encounter the morale of the story. It was patience that he made me count. The patience that God beholds towards us and even the prophets who couldn't accumulate forgiveness for the lady.

For the first time in life with me, dad made an effort to count the patience that he beholds. Far lesser than what God beheld but far in amounts to what humans behold.

He had chosen patience over so many things.

He for the first time gave me a lesson face to face.

Suddenly I remembered the 5 o'clock morning, after prayer hadiths in the mosque that I sat to listen alongwith dad but I hadn't really mindfully listened to it.

The *maulana* had read out, "God has asked for two things in his book—namaz and patience"

We ate samosas carousing in the taste hinting no story told, no lesson learnt and no patience counted.

It was all in a flash off gone moment thing. He had given me the lesson and I had quietly learned it.

Dad was making me learn disputable things. When I considered him a bad inspiration, I wasn't totally wrong.

The problem that he never masticated was that he had lived his life and I had yet to live it.

The knowledge, the prodigies he was making me learn could all be very tough for me to hold on forever.

My uncle sometimes ran away swiftly when too much of wisdom matters were being telecasted in the television. Upon askance by mom, he laughed and said, "You know, knowledge we learn is a responsibility. If what you have learned can't be retained into implication, it is a sin." So, he had chosen to attain less knowledge to gain lesser responsibilities.

I was stuck with time. Probably, when I would have reached to age 40, I would have only then realized what things did I miss at my prime age that I should have done.

Dad's finest advice among so many had always been, "Of not being able to do a certain thing" was really a satirical form of life.

I had to make a move. The time though was flowing but was stuck on me.

Late at night after the dinner, I finally gutted to make an effort.

I was an aspirant for Delhi University but I hadn't succeeded. I had to look for other place now and dad was the one to tell me.

I requested mom to convey dad that the admission time might get over everywhere if we approach too late from here onwards. It was conveyed.

Dad called me in his room after we had our regular dinner and all.

I was pressing his legs in an ambient light atmosphere. For a diabetic patient as him, it was usual to have been occupied in that tearing pain every other night. He had a customized tactic to keep talking to me all the while I was pressing his legs so that Amen doesn't feel fatigued with the act.

On those time, whatever I talked, all was in my favor. Whatever I asked or talked on these moments were probably 'yes' from the other side.

Two things but I feared always.

One—the immediate reaction of any man not only dad on strange talk.

Second—with dad, he was very adamant to the first answers that he gave. If he said 'No' it for a long time meant to be no without any compromises.

This time the question was thrown by him making me feel relieved to the first tension-phase of the talk.

"What have you thought Amen?" queried a soft, quivering and a dim voice.

"You know I've always wanted to go Delhi from so before." I said promptly.

"What's now to be done?" dad asked back sharply, straight to the point, lessening the quotient of dimness, notifying me the try that I have already given for Delhi.

I wasn't expecting this. I had thought to take advantage of the dim state of voice that he was smearing with, but he had shimmered and awoken abruptly.

I shut my mouth thereon till dad felt asleep with the pressing of legs throwing back the stark realization of independency signifying 'the decision is all yours'

Father's mild snoring at his sleep, semi darkness of the room, swooshing sound from the ceiling fan and the finishing off to another hectic day looked so perfectly peaceful with the environment on dad's face.

I went to my room dazzling at the liberty of my own decision that was to be taken. As I opened the door of my room and switched on the lights, all those glued up lights especially the 200watt bulb just above the mirror which I had suffixed for a fairer view of my own face glowed to the sensory department of my mind with a morale to an enlightened story that 'You are your king'
Once again, all the options in world were re-opened. Dad had screeched aloud 'the ball is in your court'
It wasn't easy though. All consequences for good or bad was now upon me. That night I managed to sleep somehow purely unwell.

I called many cousins at different places for their suggestion on my further studies with a view point that someone might offer invitingly to his city to come study here but nobody took a step forward in this direction rather everybody had the best suggestions but just not in favor for their own cities.

Meanwhile, we had a match with the Y.C.C, the ever-born rivals to us. All this time, I had grown as an elite player of Gurans Cricket Club, an opener bowler with lots of faith in the lower order batting position with an impression to crumble the oppositions with the last minute hitting of boundaries.
It was the semifinal of the tournament. I was batting well in the tournament, being man of the match the previous game. I was entrusted to go up in the first-down batting order to set up a huge score. But,

with over-ambitiousness of the responsibility and the entrustment of team members, I was no responsible at all. Very quickly, just on five runs I was back to the pavilion.

We set 119 to chase in 20 overs. Bowling was my responsibility. Taking wickets of the top notches was my duty. I took the opener but other players quite firmly affixed to their places in the middle.
I was desperate for win as it should have been; I wasn't unmindfully patriotic but mindfully passionate.

The wickets had fallen in the middle of the game but with very less effect. When it needed 17 out of 18, I chipped in taking one more wicket making it 15 on 12. My limited overs had finished. I was the hero, I was the acting captain, I was the king.
Deciding next two bowlers was a hard decision. Next over, two boundaries and couple of runs was hit to the leg spinner to whom I had entrusted so much, leaving the ball at 5 to win from 6 balls.
No other option than to encourage Paras for the last over. I believed in magical turnovers in cricket. It wasn't a magic required but not very less to it.

First two balls went in dot due to orthodox field setting accompanied with exceptional fielding by the boys. We bucked up like giants, we sledged batsmen like rowdies, we eagled up to the ball like devotees.
One run was taken on the third ball. Fourth ball saw a wicket in the hands of Paras.
I bumped and bounced in the air proportional to the rejoice of the wicket taking moment. I had never seen so big gap between ground and my legs that were flying on

the air. We were enthralled to have been smelling victory from a match that was not at all ours from the beginning. Everybody jumped up to the catcher, rolled up the bowler, mangled the fluffy hairs.

Next, In came was a lefty batsman. Paras bowled a wide. Fifth ball went for two runs and the match already tied, last ball demanded one for victory.

I was talking to the bowler but his body language demeaned victory conveying with an exhausted face 'whatever you tell me buddy, I can't make you win this match'

I knew we would lose. When Paras bowled the final delivery, lefty batsman so easily stepped out of the crease and hit a boundary up from the extra covers as if he was teasing us and had taken the game till the last ball just to resent us.

We had lost the match yet again. I had grown but the haunts of bad words from others had yet not left its shade on pronouncing 'we lost' Yassar's sister had well given up the taunts of cricket but on losing; the taunts symphonizing of many voices always reached my ears.

One more block of lie could be thrown to asking people that we had won but next morning the newspaper would confirm our lost to Y.C.C so it was useless as well.

In all, failing had not left my robe at anytime. It was small nitpicks that I was getting failed in but it was altogether amassing into a bigger version of failureness that was to be seen.

The only thing that I hadn't failed as yet was me. This was my only positive point.

I had always faith in myself. I had yet not failed myself. I had an easier option always available to leave all those things where I had a probability to fail. I had a father's industry, work as an employer there, enjoy all the relishing in the set-up but I had chosen things the harder way.

When I played cricket matches, I basically stood on the grounds of 50-50 chances of winning or losing. I knew that.

Losing in small matches of this place, I was dreaming about playing from one of the world's hardest stage: Indian Cricket Team.

I had not yet lost the capability to dream. Failureness had yet not broken me to think of wonders that I could do. I might fail again but I dared to fail again.

But whatsoever and howsoever I might make the fuss of failing look good, it was all very pathetic and chillingly insane.

When I had failed in my grades and dad had cried with the disappointment I had given, I was the clumsiest ever human being felt.

On those days, I had my minds in all direction. I was looking like hawk for sources of earning money. Rich people who are now worldly famous had started working early in an unusual fashion like they had left up studies very early or things like this.

One of my old childhood friend who was lost for so many years met upon one day as he was back in this old town. He had taken up father's travelling business with the support of his elder brother who was a mechanic; giving services in embassies, hotels and banks.

Through him, I got to know that he had taken an order for 500 pieces of sports shoe.

I didn't know how would have I done it but I approached and convinced my friend Vaibhav to let me try and fulfill the order. The only space that he had left was he needed shoes in the lowest price possible.

I had seen that space and had convinced him for the same.

I got the order. I phoned Ezel and he directly sent samples priced on the factory rate. Three shoes were sent, I gave that to my friend and he finalized the order.

It was so simple.

It was so very simple. The net profit cutting all the transportation and custom cost was to be 30,000.

Oh God! What was I to do of so much money. I was enthralled to have just the thought of so much money on my hands and how shall I distribute it.

I sat with my mother in the portico. I relayed her the whole work and progress going on. I told to her—10 percent must go to the mosque for renovation, it needs a whole lot of repairing. Secondly, I'll bring a tread mill in home for that everybody needs to exercise a bit and I'll bring you a gold bangle from the profits.

Mom's little stretching smile was visible to me. She wasn't saying anything so that I don't get discouraged with any of the acts. But she very well knew the floor of building that I was mounting and structuring in the air.

She wrinkled her eyebrow on hearing the amount—30,000. It was a big act from me at my age. Her stretched smile was growing uncontrollable at my more and more plans of the money that hadn't arrived yet.

Probably when building the castles in the air went beyond limits to the enduring audibility of mother, she wrinkled her eyebrow even more higher.

She looked upward, I felt awkward and she spoke in a slow motioned fashion with the stretched smile, which had now turned into a full swing laugh, *"Mungerilal ke haseen sapne"* I was serious with my talks but her smile had taken away all the humdrums of existing matters in this world. It was one of the cleanest smiles capsulated, one of the earnest presentation of the face and the truest reaction of a mother.

I too laughed out loud on hearing—'*Mungerilal ke haseen sapne*'

That work never happened.

Here, Dad was sewing his own line of advises. It looked perfect in the practical world for dad to clutch the hands of Amen studying and working in this place. Morning from 6 to 12 in the college and later half of the day in the factory. The factory had every chance of growing big but "what about Amen," I asked from a sullen heart.

How many times do we echo our heart in pursuit of the dream that we need to cherish and the echo looks so fanciful and good that we keep on echoing constantly uncaring to listen the reverted sound and the reply of it. This was the fashion of the newer world—You do it or not, you have to be chanting beautiful words.

Hooking up at the same place and looking after the factory wasn't a bad idea in view of a stabilized life of

Amen but for the bigger scoping masters, it was a bad idea, very bad idea, infact near to self crime.

It wasn't at all appropriate.

Couple of days went on and dad could read the quotients of confusion residing on my face.

He suggested me to further study at Imperial College of Management in Biratnagar itself.

His suggestion was a blank page. Any of my dreams weren't shattered yet, only its wings were being cut down.

The wings would cut down at the cost of complete shuddering closed eyes to the dream of Indian Cricket Team. Eyes closed to the future of journalism as well because of not-so good colleges here in this field.

If I was confused then people ought to be suggesting me, that was no evil thing. Though implication of sayings were quite very difficult.

Father's advice at studying Biratnagar wasn't taken.

I with lots of doubt was finally landing up in Kathmandu. Literally, it wasn't all to be called as 'a dream cherished' but it was a kind of 'what to do . . . what to do?' and suddenly someone had shown me something to do.

I was to stay with Adnan. He showed me the best management college—KCM which was probably going to be my landing up station while he had picked me from airport for the first time.

I saw it with lots of admiration, lots of thought and with lots of decision that was to be administered.

I was now realizing that dad was guzzling me to a place strictly where some guardian was settled up. Adnan was a man chasing his dreams, 'his own dreams'

Away from parents, I was realizing my individuality. Ever since I had failed, I had strongly believed on whatever happened was penultimate towards a finer cause.

The college was too expensive.

For Adnan, when a man goes out to chase a very big dream, he adopts too many things with the fakeness. Fake show-off, Fake principles, Fake money buzz, Fake fashion icon, Fake friendships and many many things in pursuit to level up the statement of the big people.

Adnan was growing as one more hooligan in the fake society.

I gave the internal exams and followed rest of the procedures with interviews and other tests which were just a show off by the college administration to make us believe that it was hard and tough to get in this college. They only sought to increase the hungerness of famished people.

I was following everything to grow same into the fashion as everyone else was doing. On all this while, I had stopped listening to my heart where earlier I condensed God to have been living there, talking and telling things that were to be done.

To say in a good language—it was sensible thoughts and meticulous planning that I was more into. I had stopped listening to my heart seriously.

I was now blank to have any dream. My whole set of plans were disturbed; neither was I doing journalism nor was I vying for the Indian Cricket Team.

The ground where I stood was now very small. The remainders of whatever big I achieved at this place was worthless.

Getting admitted in the best management college, paying that heavy fees, getting the laptop was all momentarily deceiving.

I shouldn't have been smiling so much as if I was so happy rather I should have been thoughtful for where I had finally landed up. Certainly, there are weak moments where we are robbed by seemingly 'wonderful' pieces of time.

I was robbed, I was despaired and I was crippingly new.

I attended the orientation of 3 days. I was trying to create new dreams and achievements that I should have looked to achieve hereon but I was blank. From here on, basically I was carrying a 'blank dream'

If I consulted to some logical man, he would make me know that there is no such thing as blank dream. Either there is a dream or you are blank. It was true, how could I have a blank dream.

But I was no dull and there are always different views of perception. Justification to the term 'blank dream' was that I knew, I had to achieve something big 'whatever be it' but I didn't know what it was.

It wasn't my duty to make everybody understand the philosophy of blank dream or convince them about the same but it was a heaved pressure to show everybody that here lives a man called Amen.

First day in college was nothing more than any other day during school. It was usual. There was shyness in everybody I met, eyeing the heavy-weighted people who probably could be near competitor in the coming college times, categorizing and bordering the not-so-interesting girls from the beautiful pieces, displaying the quotients of coolness to everybody and selecting a group that could be suitable to get alongwith.

Sometimes back I had never stepped inside a moving bus. Here, I had to change two tempos to get home. I was stunned to find amazing differences of emotions. I was liking the newness of everyday travelling in a tempo. In tempo, I would get lost with so many things that I countered in the busy roads. I watched people attentively, I peeped in their eyes closely, inside their intense struggle and their perspiration to get the most basic ingredient: food

Sometimes, I realized everybody had a story to tell.

The introspection inside every eye tonged a new kind of embezzlement.

The struggle was very hard for everybody. It wasn't a long call needed but only exemption from one time of meal that could lead them to dishonesty, two times of meal that could lead them to stealing, one day of hungry sleep could have led them to cheating. It wasn't a long call needed at all.

On the other end, when I reached home from college, Adnan would all the time be ready with his showcase of strength in words for discipline. Probably for him, home cleaning and college were the only things that I was worth of. Back in the mind, this reason of mindset was his impression on me of a failure. And for a failure, reaching even to the half level of upgradation in life was an achievement, this was the perception of people.

I beared all that with intensity, intensity of struggle. I had never forgotten that Dad wasted his four years before he settled his own industry and so he valued the brand of industrialist that he had achieved. When he gave that up in separation, he was again intensified to struggle for the re-settling on the same stature.

Achievement without struggle is a one hand man, and with struggle, achiever's both hand pop out suddenly because then he knows the graciousness of an achievement.

This was not my place.

When I was in 12th, I had thought of choosing an easy course and getting on with my dreams but everything had completely changed. I had come to the wrong place, chosen a tough course of BBA and I had changed my dream into a blank one.

My business of mind was all captured with studies and sometimes unwanted parties thrown by college.

Then, how was I to reconcile, how was I to reconcile the wrong that had happened?

I felt clumsy everyday to struggle. However good the word 'struggle' sounded, the bad thing about patiently bearing the pain is that at times it makes us fearful for what if life will drip to an end with the same course of patience, constantly bearing the same thing.

Sometimes it was necessary to cut patience from the trend and be impatient to the hard times, sometimes it was important to make an end to the sorrows burnt, sometimes it was important to be impatient.

Yes, impatience was the plan-B, the substituted language, heeding its necessity to get learnt.

The college wasn't bad. I was learning new and worrying things. I didn't know that BBA was unofficially a half course and MBA was needed to make it full. I didn't know management was basically managing; that's it, nothing else! I didn't know that we would be taught here to get a job 'anyhow' and earn money, that too after MBA.

I was rightly afflicted to pursue journalism but I was wrongly fussed up with management.

Humans think too much but implement little. Heart shows the path too far but mind walk in it too little. Ambition stark and reaches sky but fear masks the whole idea to burial ground.

The simplicity of the problem was that—I was not satisfied where I was, what I was becoming and so I needed to change things according to my own convenience but the complexity of problem was that how was I to change everything NOW?

My life, if seen from a mediocre angle was fine. But, if seen from Amen's eyes, that had now turned visionary, it did breed on a very small piece of land.

I had no problems at all.

A friend's bike cornered everyday at 6 o'clock in the morning waiting for me and peeping the horn in agony. I attended college till 11.30 then we went to the canteen, sipping tea and other boys smoking. At around 12.30 or 1.00 in the afternoon, the same bike-fellow dropped me to home. At home, cleaning and updating things in finely order to get saved from Adnan's staunching words were my whole busy-ness of the mind.

Work and leisure both finished off for the day, then would my time start to think about the dissatisfactions I was facing and the dilemma would grow bigger and bigger until the night would approach and I would give up all thoughts of changing things and would wake up in the same delusion on the other day.

This was my pleasure in the lexicon of daily life and perhaps this was to be my schedule for many more days to come.

I had seen people tight with their schedules, scared and anxious to future, making lots of preparation to get a good job and a settled life.

From ever before, I had never thought of gaining a degree for the sake that it would make me land into a settled life. I had to learn many things on the while I was attaining a degree. Human's caliber was dependent upon nothing except his own will power, and education instilled that will power, Really it did . . .

I wasn't ready to construct my settling up of future to the bachelor's degree that I would earn after bruising and burying whatever little mind I had left.

The thought of universalism always stroked my mind. Though hard to find practicality but I believed that everybody had the same potent to control their own lives. It wasn't about a bachelor's degree holder or a non-degree holder. Everyone of us could construct their own weight of responsibility to the fall of achievement.

But wait!!

What was I thinking at this point of time?
Was I making grounds to remain bachelor-less in terms of degree?

Where was that thing called . . . life!!
I had not seen much parts of the world.
I wanted to live into the wild like AlexanderDumes, I wanted one hell of a titanic freelance time like Jack Dawson, I wanted to be rough and rude and tough like the characters from Johnny Cash lyrics, I wanted to be a mindful con genius shouting at the whole blot of chasers 'Catch me if you can' I wanted to be in solidarity casted away from the whole world as if trapped in a distant unreachable island like Tom Hanks, Most recently, I wanted to feel the pursuit of happiness like Christopher.

Apart from those Hollywood inspiring flicks, there were sad realities to follow. There were five exams in one semester, four internals, one central exam which was the main one. We were made to accept every exam with the same sanction of hardwork and any red marks in the subject was dealt with same severity.

There was also a group I belonged to—'*soom*'
I from the first day never got to know on what was this name kept but I always acted as I knew
We were eight members. All were strangled in bikes except me, cushioned with lots of father's monetary back up but they never tried to make me feel any uncomfortable and it was on these moments of comforting me that I felt uncomfortable.

With the same schedule and hopping of the same dissatisfactions, I gave the 1st semester central exams after 6 months. There was no point in talking about the internal ones because I gave a damn to them.

On the hour when results were to be out, notice board area was suddenly the sensationalized part of the building, sobbing had already started in advance for some girls as assumptions were hugely made.

When the results actually came, I was more comfortable watching people and their reactions from a 20 meter distance. Maybe I was to be the worst performer in these semester exams but it was more encouraging to see these people's faces before I actually saw mine.

I was dismayed with myself to find the same identical fear on seeing results even after so many years of studying. I questioned myself, "Would I be hanging in this cliff all my life and attain a degree in the very same fashion?

Was this going to be the achievement of my life—to have passed bachelors-somehow?"

I wanted to be of those happy members on seeing results, I wanted to go home and commandingly show my grade results to my family which unfortunately had never happened.

I wanted to be like one of the members from *soom* group who so easily sat down in classes, joked like all of us and silkily passed on with the best grades.

I hadn't yet flipped through the notice board. Talking to oneself is always a better option because you can say just anything to yourself without any reproach.

People around me were new, so many years of schooling was over.

It was a new incarnation of me at this new place among new people, I had the chance to make a newer impression among these new group of people as well.

Now, if I went to find my 7digit roll number anywhere near to the notice board area, people would come to know in some way or another for what I have scored and my stature could again go in the same sorryful state.

The hippy display infront of '*soom*' group that the result will be fine was all fake.

I was reluctant to see the scores sensing what the notice board at some heart punch of it would have beheld for me. 'Its alright' I said to my bruising heart with a sinking tone as the last declaration of hope.

It wasn't!

It wasn't alright!!

I viewed the result. I had passed in all but I could not score the minimum GPA required. I could not score 2 GPA, got stuck on 1.96

Deep down, I sighed, "thank God"

I was satisfied.

And as I said, thank god on such a result, the *soom* group came to know my status. I saw their eyes, they were bursting with a question, "are you such pathetic in studies?"

I laughed, chilled and went on gleeful for rest of the day.

I was now required to give GPA make up examination in somewhere around 2 months later.

'who cares for the examination that is after 2 months, huh!'

The conclusion was that I had not failed, though I had not passed as well but 'I hadn't failed' remained the more emphasized sentence.

It did not matter much to my guardians if I was passing or failing until and unless I discontinued going to college because that was their assurance point.

I was now enrolled into the 2nd semester. I could feel the exhaustion in such quick time in the college premises, deeply stirring to a thought—'Are things going to be like this always?

I could now go on believing that I had no chance of being satisfied at achievement of anything. I was in the best management college of Nepal, best university badged up and with the best group available—*soom*

What more was needed to get in the honor of satisfaction?

But, I wasn't

It was larger amount of courage needed to take a stronger decision than I actually had. I was always ready to relive the thought of leaving everything and going towards the dreams that I had set but all those things only looked happening in some moments of thought now.

To implement courageous thoughts, we need to be at the helm of a courage.

Ok. Everything aside. I doubted even if leaving everything could have proved a courageous act or not.

Maybe, it couldn't. The definition said 'you're running away'

Our group liked exploring places in an unplanned way and that was really the best way. We went to the highest altitude of the capital, from where it was supposed that

Kathmandu looked at its unimaginable beauty. The height was known as 'palanchowki' path was steep and tough, something that gave you a feeling of 'struggle and achievement'

Most of the Nepali writers must have sat down at this place and wrote those beautiful pieces of literature.

Kathmandu was a real distinct piece of place in this world. There was something very special about pronouncing 'I am at United World Trade Centre' as a kid when I had come to Kathmandu but now there was everything casual about the same thing summed up as 'near to WTC'

Foreigners were seen with so much of excitement but seeing them every now and then stranding in the valley, they looked like one of us.

People speaking english in even simple conversation was now no highly educated people's tantrum but the need of every commoner.

After exams, vacations normally popped up.

On the first vacation, when I was heading towards home, my small town hadn't looked more endearing as today. It was now that I discovered an aroma in the air that my town had in itself and that the scent was romantically sent for me.

It was an overnight journey from Kathmandu to my place. I wasn't anything sensitive as to get into the flunk of home-sickness, although the awaitness was hitting high on that day to get back home undisturbed to the usual bounces and discomfort on the rickety bus.

I changed from emotional songs to very emotional songs on my earphone looking outside the window, air breezing on me, purring on my hair onto the eardrums like my mom slowly scrabbling the ear holes and putting me into bottomless ever-secured sleep.

When I awoke from a deep sleep at 5.30 in the morning, I was at the highway of my home. I didn't know that after 6 months when I would have come home, it was hard to even spot your own road in which you had travelled innumerous stretches.

The three lanes that distinguished heavy vehicle from cycle and rickshaw lane to motorbike lanes was all submerged into one big highway that had made its identification difficult, the maternity hospital at the opposite side of the road which screeched importance to all the women in the town was transformed into a glassy tall building of B class development bank, the not so happening barber shop just beside it had remodeled its door-face with black reflective glass screaming to all the wayfarers with a reflection 'see, how ugly you look!!come in, we'll groom and transform you'

Opposite to the barber's well advertising shop stood an army of lethargy rickshaw pullers to whom their wives had probably sent them forcing to earn and they had chosen this place as an escape.

There was misfortune in their stars, laziness in their work and still an affirmed look to earn money so that they don't go home with the night session of beating and quarrels at their home.

I took a rickshaw though it was 5 minutes walking distance. The resplendent blue gate of my home with little spots of rustiness in the iron was visible from far distance, the white arch happening to be the favorite design directed by dad on the gate was gleaming and bouncing with the coming of my rejoice. Ten rupees paid to the rickshaw and I opened my gate for the entry.

I walked the garden scenic distance, clearly mom and Sheezan had yet not given up their appetite for decoration, van looked steadily performing as yet, standing at its affixed portico place with white shining body.

The morning had its own charm of a satisfying look. Mom had been waiting for me, dad yet asleep.

'Wow!' I exclaimed with bowels and lungs bumping out with excitement.

What should I do for them? In this little time of 15 days that I have come to spend at home, what should I do for them?

Should I press their legs all night till they don't fall asleep? Should I buy all the best vegetables and fruits from the market that mom always wanted me to bring? Should I with all my efforts keep on helping mom with the household chores that she is addicted on doing? Should I do all the petite running here and there jobs of my father making myself look into some use? What should I do?

I was now an adult, my mom made it know when she served me tea and not milk. I said "strong tea please" making her know about the variations of the drink that I know now.

I tried to watch her face as deep as possible trying to find the wrinkles that age must have brought upon but thank God, she was not old as yet. She was fit and fine, not crouching upon anything, neither stooped on back, henna well applied on hair, maintaining the rigidness of 'not an oldie as yet'

I still had more time to earn lots of money until my parents would have trickled down to ageing and then, there would have been my stronger role of helping them.

I entered my room that stood second on the right. The door was still properly polished. Bracket tubelight had lost its bracket and maybe the light also. Yes, when I switched on, tubelight was fused as well. Fan had collected heap of dust on itself giving me a dismal shame of justification 'What!! I haven't been used for quite long now'

Sleeping was always a tranquilizer. I woke up on the afternoon, things looked casual as to my days when I used to be here. The feeling of helping anyone at home was gone as it never had approached.

The days were simple. Dad had his own worries, mom had her own and Sheezan had his own. Everybody had their own and I had mine personal as well. Ofcourse, I was now a grown-up and I had to have them.

Nobody sans worries in this world!!

So, what was to worry.

Days had changed and so had generations as it looked. Nobody was younger these days, with everyday changing technologies, even a 19 aged teen could look out of fashion sometimes.

Truly, technology never remains new and young.

At this while of holidays, my email inbox was fluttering with emails—'Anita, Ishan, Rahul, bla bla has invited you to join facebook'

Ever since, I had seen Faiza scrabbling with social networking site as orkut just for the sake to tiptoe the fashion with people, this act of her always daunted me to be out of this belief.

But time had changed, I did not want to be an oldie. Faiza was neither interested nor was she here to check if I was still onto my principles or not.

I first logged on to facebook, my gawd!!

I was the latest person to arrive on it. Already people had 80, 90, 200 or even 500 friends, the number of friends led to know the man's status.

My busy-ness of mind was to sit and scheme for how to increase the friend's number fast and quick.

Stepping inside any cyber café viewed loads of people with facebook skin on their screens, checking out cool status' of people and finding friends, friends of friends or however far they could reach until they lost the chord of a mutual friend.

The achievement that I was making in this 15 days of stay at home was that—I had stringed 84 friends already and many more were in the pipeline. I was able to buckle up from oldest friends to the newest; all at one place with no privacy and complete transparency. Facebook was so cool.

So what!!

This was the question, when fire for facebook lulled down little.

What was so remarkable about it? Was I not losing myself to the fashion of the world; but how could have I resisted alone if the whole world chanted 'this is fashion, either you are with us or left back time ago very much like you had missed the train in your painting' There was something special about not using the phrase 'against us' because there was no point in it. I could not have run the show alone or in solidarity.

This was the time when photos were clicked for the sake that it shall be uploaded by evening on facebook, quotations were searched for the sake that it shall be my today's status, wall posts and comments were posted for the sake that somebody would 'like' it.

My 15 days of stay was getting over. I did nothing remarkable in between this time. I did nothing or not even anyway near to what I had thought to do when I had come home to spend vacations.

There are some moments when you grow passionate even you can kill somebody and there are some moments when you become so dull even to react on the same frame of situation. We just get robbed down with frames of moment.

I was back again at Kathmandu swayed down like a pendulum, who had dwindled to the extreme right and after 15 days of stay at home I was back again at the extreme left. There was no lexicon or perhaps nothing energetic around. I was clotted to simply sway from one side to another in the same string without any power to change what was needed to be changed.

We have one hundred definitions to any act, good or bad! Its only how we would like to see and how we would like to interpret the matter.

I often regarded my dull life as struggle and sometimes 'intense struggle'

Sometimes I even called it patience and often I called it 'patiently bearing'

But when I became harsh to my thoughts, I realized that I may just be pretending to change the language, trying to sound good of a bad illustration.

First semester was over here. I stated 'seven semesters left' Then I condensed 'three and a half years'
For sure, I shouldn't have chosen BBA at any cost at this land atleast where 4 years was needed to become a commerce graduate.
And that too people blotted that around as 'an unofficial half degree' completed, MBA needing to make it full.
That meant 4 years plus 2 years completely made it unbearable to hang around.
Even here, the humdrum to pay hefty fee existed.
Whatever we did, however we did, God made this hundred percent sure that we will reach to death. The in-between of life and death is amazing to have; I don't know how was I sculpting this in-between thing but I had to be dead sure about carving it in absolute direction.

The starting of second semester didn't bring any excitement. During school days, atleast new students came in with the new session.
There were slide shows in the projector, there were best available faculty, there were kind and unkind people alike everywhere, there were opportunities, competitions, all sorts of juggling material but where was that thing called life!!
It was like a stand-up comedian reading his script and suddenly he puts up the most strange line of having forgotten to have lived his life.

There are certain times when we really do realize what we want and so we can't go on pretending forever 'this is the life we have wanted'

Time kept passing by.

One day before the internal exams of second semester, there was a 'good' problem that arrived. My second installment were due since one and a half months and internal exams were a good medium for the college administration to recover the left out fees from the students otherwise not allowing them to appear in the exams.

A play presentation was going on during English class; when a black, half bald peon in his blue uniform pushed the door softly respecting the presence of a professor. He found me at one glance, connected to my eyes, rudeness and authority was audible at his walk of 10 meter distance towards me. I came to know the value of a millimeter and microsecond.

On that flicker of moments, I was negotiating with destiny to lengthen the walk of the peon, to stretch the passage of time, something miraculous happens and he never gets to reach me and embarrass me.

'The long walk to freedom' might have conceded 27 years of Nelson Mandela's life but this longest walk that I was seeing wasn't even 27 seconds far away.

Everything was paused. I wished Faiza to suddenly come here and start playing 'statue' with him.

Embarrassment was faced.

I talked to professors, administration; it was an embarrassing matter to talk about as it was a rich college laden with rich students, and even if somebody wasn't rich here, he had to pretend rich.

Adnan was called as a local guardian. He was phoned and informed that your cousin can't appear for the exams scheduled from tomorrow.

He preconceived looking at my background that he must not have passed the required standards academically needed to appear in the examinations.

He came to the college, I hadn't told him a thing about the fee matters because I was trying on my own to fulfill by writing articles for a newspaper as I had done in the first semesters but all plannings had failed, as many of my articles were rejected this time.

He talked to the professor and then he came to know about my fees problem.

He sat in the waiting lounge, I companied him.

He was silent, I companied him with silence.

It wasn't only embarrassing to talk with professors for some more time but it was also embarrassing to talk with this guy Adnan—he was a cousin afterall.

I was thinking loads of things. I had some attitude and ego; but here I was: head down, asking as a beggar if you could help me to Adnan. All for what!

For a thing that I don't want to do at all.

"It isn't worth it," I essayed to myself.

Nevertheless it was a good problem because it was that moment when I decided to discontinue my bachelors study and pursue what I had always thought to do.

"I have finally decided. It took me more than five years," I declared to myself sitting on the couch.

Though the fee amount was paid but what for. I failed in 2 subjects again. Did I give everybody so much of tension only to get failed.

Things weren't worth what was happening.

I had finally decided this. As the second semester which was of four months duration gets completed, I shall drop out.

This was a time when I searched all the int'l drop-out people in the internet.

All night I jingled up the most emphasized sentences from famous speeches of drop-outs.

Steve Jobs—"Truth be told, I never graduated from a college"

Bill gates—"I have been waiting for more than 30 years to say this—Dad, I always told you, I would come back and get my degree"

Often all night, I kept searching in google—"List of famous drop-outs"

And the names would come from Tom cruise, Jim Carrey, Albert Einstein to Dhirubhai Ambani, Raghu Ramalingam.

Most of the listed people were Americans but I didn't mind until they gave me good encouragement.

In short, there were 8 U.S presidents without bachelors degree, 10 Nobel prize winners, 62 Oscar winners, 55 best-selling authors and uncountable millionaires.

The decision had come onto me—I was going to drop-out after second semesters.

How cool did it sound—'Drop-out by choice'

I carefully never shared my decision with anybody. Second semester hopped in, I gave the exams quietly as I had no plans ahead and as if I would have shuffled into 3rd semesters silkily . . . who knew anyways, I had greater plans ahead.

Only '*soom*' group had the hint of me leaving college after the exams get over. A small party was thrown for me—dinner, night out, etc.

This gave a little more stern and a responsible look to affix the dropping out determination.

Four months was past. I dropped-out.

I always sub consciously thought about this but finally today I had taken the decision, I had dropped out.

It was a big decision from me, a real difficult one asking me to go only one way now—stronger . . .

Convincing dad was difficult, telling mom was easy and making brothers understand was an ordeal.

But I had gone stronger . . . Sorry people!!

I was not a rebellion exactly. Many a times nobody bothered to talk flip side of the story in any way, we generally talked what we wanted to say and what the other wanted to hear.

People who had now reached success advertised their tales of failureness so vividly that they had seen in such and such part of life only when they had reached to the easier cushion of success. Nobody dared to speech out at the while they were struggling. The harder path walked by people in stories were only conveyed if they reached to the easier cushion. Never were their stories relayed who lost the battle in mid-way, who might have given up too very early or who might have failed and failed and might have given up in that constant fiasco.

I went back home after giving the second semester exams, results who cared for now!
For next one month at home, time hadn't looked so strict before.
It was one of the most difficult time that I had faced.
I thought for many days, how to carry out things now?

I couldn't have said to dad about my plans straight-away. I couldn't have said, "now, I want to try for Indian Cricket team"
I thought and thought, and gave dad only this statement—"To tell yourself that you can do something, we don't really need the fuss of a degree"
"Amen isn't interested in attaining a degree," that is what dad understood in simple terms conveying mom.

Chapter-8

On 10th of september, 2006, I wrote the letter.
I had always stopped myself from doing this act because this was always gonna be the last step before leaving home.

So was I ready for this now?

Yes, I was

Uhhh, Yes I was

Maybe,

Naa

No, I wasn't

I had failed for the first time in ninth class and that was the time when this concept of letter was born. From that time onwards till today, it has continued to fade in and fade out hinting as it is now a hobby to hop up thinking such way. Six years of continuous delay sterned its voice that now was the time to no-delay. At this junction of life, 2nd semester studies done, looked as the administering time of a long awaited halt.

"Yes, now is the time!" I marked to myself the importance of delivering this sentence alike Martin Luther King Jr's most emphasized sentence in his famous speech. I roared and announced to myself again—'Now, is the time'

So how was I to start things off, what was the procedure?

I took two days of time from myself to see if this was the final declaration or would have I again changed the thought.

I was embroiling everything into the account of my decision, i.e. How hard thoughts and cry would my parents give?

Would this act give even more burden to my family?

Would everybody get more tangled in searching for me or would people settle down after some amount of search saying, "Ok, let's wait for one year as Amen has asked?"

And the most important thing—would have my decision proven substantial when I would have come after one year? The last one was the most important one; that hit right on the middle of the dart. I was surprised from where did that question bump up all of a sudden and that too today at this critical time. I had always thought of leaving everything but for the first time, I was asking to myself— Would have my decision proven substantial, would have I been able to make it?

Now, it was not the 'no-determination' part ailing me but my own capability questioning. After all, really India just needed 11 out of millions. I have never won a tv, cycle or anything in coke or Fanta or sprite bottles but do I really consider myself lucky enough for this place, for this crucified place?

I looked for no answers. I wanted no answers and I had no answers.

One year was a potential time, I considered to make it two but that would have been little unsettling and longer time for my family to sit down quietly and wait.
In everything, there is little problem, always.
Nobody sans problem!
Nobody.

My set of plans were ready, the perfect planning by the not so perfect planner looked done. It was going to be Delhi. One year of time. Place untold to family. Conversation through email. Proper letter left up.
For six years, I had awaited creeping like some sort of hobby to write a letter before leaving home. As an expert, I should have run the pen onto paper like a palanquin swaying on the bearer's arm but I was worried and thoughtful for how to start, how to end and what exactly to tell.
'There is no expert method of writing a letter to your family before leaving home' I bet that!
I needed to talk with dad before I really left but talking to dad hinting that I am leaving for one year had the potentiality to change my whole mind. So better was it to let it be.
He was a persuader, able to flow anybody, even the waves in the ocean only if they could articulate but good for them that they were dumb.

I invoke some guts from interiors, waited until we finished our dinner and I sat down to talk with him. I took a position in the sofa, made myself sit straight like an army general with all proper etiquettes and readied to speak to dad, though he was still busy with the towel unrealizing and unaffected by any of my moves.

The guts suddenly tried to show back, away to an intuition that 'he is surely gonna change your mind'

"Letter would be detail and well explained" I convinced to my off distance not so gutsy heart now.

Two days had past, the lease of time for determination made things deterrent this time.

I was little fearful because there was always a flip side to any story though I wasn't ready to listen but there was another side of the coin. "What if I fail?" was the bingo question

"What if I fail?" I asked again, clearing my throat to get my voice. I heard my voice and it echoed one thousand times in ultra-slow motion onto my senses—what if you fail?

Today I had to answer this odd question, it was verifiably necessary.

"Ok. Even if I fail, I will always respect myself that I had taken the decision, and having taken a decision from a boy who had even problems on simple shopping process is a big achievement"

This was my consoling, little loopholed statement, now ready to counter in further stages of life if asked.

On third day morning, I woke before it was actually morning at 4.30. This was best time to construct a letter. Everybody asleep, only you and your thoughts.

It was now time to craft the most chunky part of the whole affair, the thumps on which the sentiments would have aroused, the surprise punch to everybody from 'an undeterred consistently failing boy' as they looked.

I sat till 5.15, writing, cutting, re-writing, re-cutting, re-structuring, re-modeling.

Finally it came!

Dad,

I have been alone my whole life and so it was only me to decide this. I know what grievance will be delivered alongwith, but this is the best thing that I and everybody else will recount in future that I had done.

It was a long process of hard decision, I have cried almost every other night lonely in a room from the time I had failed. My actual friends slipped ahead, my virtual friends giggled around and I realized them all.
For 6 years, I have thought about this, delayed presuming the tension and havoc but now was the time.

I do realize what I am giving you through this and strictly I blame no one for anything, not even me. I don't know many things. I don't know what could have been a better solution, I don't know what could have been the reconciliation, I don't know. But, I will find out. I will find out, how effective can a stamp be on man's head, how difficult can the brand of failureness be to remove. I will find and tell you what is that point of success afterall.

I will come exactly one year to this date, I will converse about my well being through emails.

Your son
Amen

I was crying from my eyes, pained from heart but an Accenture of yet amazing satisfaction. This looked to me like another catastrophic event of my life—"the boy who ran from home"

I chose Delhi again, the place from where I was dejected.
It was my firm belief that 'you succeed from where you fail'
I had left home.

When I first reached Delhi, stepped down and watched this place, I was assured to never go in a condition of no food, money or shelter because as I stepped out of the train, I saw fleets of teen boys at the railway station working at different leverages; some as a coolie, slum tourist and many of those kinds.
I clumsily boarded out of the train with one heavy bag and a travel bag on my shoulder. I paused for a couple of minutes at the boarded out piece of land, looked at each and every material for the message it could convey.
The water drinking area was clean, that showed of good managerial authority of the place. People had queued up with discipline at the ticket counter, that showed the well-being of crowd. Not many people were sleeping at the railway station, that showed a good standard.
The night wasn't looking too very dark hinting of a little source of approval from the world manager as well.

I had one year of time and I had a life to start and in a way end it as well so that I could take that form of life to my father.
I was thoughtless for where to start, how to do it though I had so meticulously planned for every pinpointed

details that I shall be doing but I was thoughtless at the practicality.

It was growing late tonight. Probably starting things off on the other day was a good idea perhaps. I had marked a whole empty bench on the very same railway platform as my place to rest for the night.

I talked to myself the whole night. I had stood thousand times all my age infront of the mirror questioning 'will I be able to do it?' that was the whole ask!

I had taken one year's time, would it be fulfilling?

It wasn't as easy; though even if I wouldn't have been able to do anything remarkable by the stipulated time, I could anytime go home, show my face and say 'Ok, I'm with you again'

That face if I ever showed up would only be compliance to blocks of failureness that I would have achieved.

How easy was everything when I had thought to leave for this journey but how adamantly and frivolously everything had started showing its other and probably truer face. The night was growing and I was thinking upon many things in my first darkness of grave seriousness.

I had thought over my bowling a ten thousand times that I was far better than any of them who had encapsulated their places in the Indian team but tonight's one thought—'you are not' shouted more authoritative.

My set of plans suggested to work in a call centre for livelihood and practice in the academy from two to six in the afternoon probably. I slept with these running thoughts.

When I woke up in the morning at the darkest hour just before the dawn, I was yet again alive. I was yet again bumming with thoughts. I was yet again ready.

The piece of cloth meant for namaz that I had kept in the convenient saggy travel bag for easy taking out and putting in gave a sense of perfect start at this new place.

When I sat on my janamaz after namaz to collect all the ideas once again in the platform, I closed my eyes for a while and I felt God's graciousness, true graciousness.

On that closed eye moment, it felt like I was not in the platform, I was in the heavens and the sea of pure milk and honey was flowing on both the sides. I could sense the effervescence, hear the fizziness, feel the foaminess and touch the bubbles of the milk. For honey, heaven's bees were surely different. I didn't know honey glittered more than gold for that I had never seen anything more pure than this. This honey looked like animation to reality and the perspiration to taste this gold looked the most lavished form of living.

I opened my eyes wide, abstracted, and with a glare. I was still in this earth; that feeling of exaltation could only have been shown from the creator.

It was clear indication of favors upon me.

With whatever spread out over the night, I recollected everything and put it into my one heavy mountain bag and the light travel bag. I headed outside the railway station. I was very afraid to make any dealings but I had to. I chose a good rickshaw fellow with the criteria fulfilling 'kind face'

With shrinking heart, I asked one rickshaw man half afraid half commanding, "I need a room on rent of around 2-3000"

"It is very tough, but I can find you one," he optimistically answered giving a hint that you have come exactly to the right person and only me from so many rickshaw men can find you a room to live.

We went in the rickshaw. I was stunned at the delightfulness of the place. The ravishing sun was just rising, sprinkling its light to here and there. Nobody enchanting salutes to this important sun-ball that had come up yet again, rather everybody immersed into the monotonous tediousness of the sun going off every night and coming back the following day. But, today for me every angle of the sun's coming up was unordinarily entrancing.

The ravishing sun had already announced of the new day that had come. People displaying the trailers for the day. Old and young with jogging apparatus had come in the show, girls and grandmas displaying their laughter classes, skull cap wearing group of people after namaz discussing and drinking tea at the corner, a little further and for some it wasn't the trailer but the work had started. Diligently and sincerely cleaning the cars, sweeping and brushing the important streets.

Yet another day in the streets had kicked off.

Looking at the room, one word was enough to describe—'clumsy'

That one room was my room and home as well, far inferior to the form of living that my dad had given to me. My dad often talked to mom that the perspiration to achieve something gives a worthiness to what you achieve. And my mom interpreted, "Your father was jobless for four years" settling up my mind that he perspired for four years before he saw his own factory.

So, it was worth what he loved.

This home was a part of my struggle, intense struggle.

Today, if I happen to meet my optional teacher who started all of this, who put me into this mind to struggle, I would thank him that it was he who had taken me out from the shells of ordinarism.

The rent was 2000. Home/room was 15x24. Everything was fine. I rested for the whole day, fearing to carry out any activity in this totally new place. I bathed, ate my last pieces of packed food from the saggy bag and slept all the while again. It was a sleep called in by the humming mistresses.

I had to set up many things inside my home. It was all empty except the floor bedding and a bucket that the landlord had provided. I took out a pen and paper from my bag, trying to note the needful stuffs that I required. It contained a pillow, mug, wall clock, broom sticks and lots of readymade snacks. That's it!

The list was too condensed and small to what I had thought it would become.

I was literally living the line, "Humans require square meals a day, few pairs of cloths and an area for shelter to sleep off"

That evening I readied for petite shopping. I stepped out of my room for the first time at this new dazzling place. I could not have protested if someone called this street as the busiest of all. I dared not to blink the eye for too long, what if I miss notable stuffs of this place. A little fear rested its clutch to the undertakings at the same time.

Delhi was a whole different place.

I walked in casualness at the streets with no hints of hurry. When one round of the area was completely seen in about an hour's time, I went inside a kitchenware store, all the noted stuffs were available at this one place. For some moments of time, I had to think like typical housewife for what things could come into use in daily homely matters.

I was back again in my room, placing the stuffs I had brought in correct spaces and slowly secluding my life to myself.

When homely matters were done and things were placed up, I diligently and swiftly came out from the mindset of a housewife, now tried to get in the module of an emotional family man.

It was 8 o'clock in the evening, second day in this place, third day since I had left home, fifth block of confusion whether to email or not, sixth row in the line of 'No, a little later' eighth flock of rush 'Yes, I should.'

I held the contest right there—Yes, I should.

I ofcourse needed to inform them of my well being.

Cyber cafes were every here and there. I again stepped out of the house and went to Communications cyber café. I opened my amen41@gmail account.

For so many years, I had always thought of writing letter to my father and leave everything. Today, finally my wish had come alive but more than a wish, today it is an in-depth cry, a belongingness to my family, an end to the awaitness of my parents' expectations. The seemingly 'hobby' wasn't any fanciful in today's time, it was a painful task.

I had thought many a times about the content of the letter when I would have left home but when I opened the compose mail section, the page wasn't the only thing blank.
I was dazzlingly thoughtful and incomparably emotional.
Email address to be sent at was of our company and so the letter first had to go from the eyes of Sheezan as he was the one who checked e-mails.

I wrote:

Bhaiya,

Today I am in no position to justify myself neither do I seek justification from anybody. I have always been alone, taken my decision on my own, this too was a part of it.

I do realize there is lot of wrong quotient to my act and what awkward position I have put you people in, especially when somebody will ask dad, "What's happening with Amen?"

But this was it!! I have cried ten thousand times looking in the mirror, I have thought 10 years from now on the time when I will look back dissatisfied at my age where I once was.

I have a dream and I don't know whether it's feasible telling you people about it. I have a failure on my back and I don't know if there is any way I can share this pain.

I will not tell you people my address, we will converse only through emails. There is no way you people can find me so put no efforts on it.
I am not unmindful of the one year time that I have taken and I am not oblivious of the things that I got to achieve.

I do realize that there was a way easier but I will try and do justice to this path chosen.

Amen

This was it—my first letter. I wasn't able to tong so much of emotional strings.
I could draw the picture of my family as they would have read this letter.

All the aside stuffs were done, now I had to get in the mainstream. I slept that night with lot of excitement.
I had marked a prestigious cricket academy to check out in the next morning.
Following morning, I went in the academy and it was Ajit Juneja's academy, one of the former players from the Indian national side.
It was an honor to be meeting this man like he had come out of the television sets to whom I had watched in my childhood days playing few but for the national side.

I was called to give my trials in the next morning at 8 o'clock. He had assigned an assistant guy to take my trials and I went with running thoughts readying myself for the next day.

Choosing Juneja's academy came with a reason that it was near to my home.

There was a herd of boys in the academy, no it was a crowd or was it a jumbled mass??

Ohh God . . .

The sort of stampeding scene was heart breaking. There were hundreds of boys, there were numbers of talent, there were the future Indian players.

They were bowling at a pace that could only discourage; batsmen were playing shots as if they had been playing those shots all day and night of their life.

Discouragement was surely a deadly disease.

I had always thought about such kind of competitions that I shall be facing but the crowd or mass, whatever it was— they were unready to let me take a leap forward infront of them. Things looked fearful. I had to better change my 'letter writing hobby' into a 'dreamer's unachieved satire'

These were my thoughts, when I was selected successfully to course my cricket with this academy.

I gazed at the whole ground, snickered at the foul game played by God, sad to the wrong judgment that had been made by me, pitied to the locked situation and in the scenario of the decision that I had once taken of leaving home. I could not go back as well. That was out of the question!

The cricket game when invented by the Britishers, Lagaan and Iqbal which had hit right on the motivational quotients of mind, WasimAkram's history of direct entry in the national team without having played even a first class match explicating bowling as a form of art and Tendulkar's young zeal and sheen in the international arena was the reason why I was transpired into this game.

All those events were stipulated and directed by God to have captured me in this trap at today's date.

The game of cricket in its establishment was all done for me, cricket had awaited in all it's time of invention for me. People from all countries had creeped in with bat and bowl all their life because some day Amen was to come into this entrapment.

Very quickly, I was looking at my third catastrophic event of life.

Was I cheated by the lord up above?

Though I was selected, I had an ocean to cross without the hint of legs attached to my lower part of the body.

The intense struggle that I had chosen at some part of time in a challenging mode with a view that 'I could turn every challenge on my side' shouted—It was just a point where you were deceived.

I was not ready to give my judgment in this initial period, seriously hoping for myself to be wrong at this point of thought.

How did people say—"whatever God did was for good"

They should look at me. They should look at this small group of heavyweight people which happens to be a fraction share of what aspiring India contends in the cricketing sector.

They should look at these coaches who expect the best from these heavyweights.

The counselors, motivation gurus, pundits of ages, visionaries, all should come in this space of ground—space of mine and look from my eyes. They were fake, they had lied all their time of life on saying 'you could do anything' or atleast they should confront that they were misinformed—"It is only sun that rises the next day not a failed man"

My body was peppering with sweats, heart beating like punches, mind working like an insane, emotions whining like a schoolboy, feet adamantly unmoved like a frozen horse and thoughts pumping like a loser.
Teachers were right when they had failed me, uncle was right when he had pierced the notion.

I stood their piercing the scene until one friendly old hand patted on my shoulder—"Amen?"
I turned back to find one of not so important members from the mills playground—"Ayan"
Oh my God, there was less amount of reactions when I had failed and I needed to go home.
There was much more moving in my head when I saw this guy.
Oh my god!

I was stunned and a zillion things came running onto mind like it had mixed all into my blood—one thought one vein.
All veins carrying a different question.

Where have you been?
How are you here?
Are you Ayan?
What did you do from the time you left Biratnagar?
So many . . .

Amen . . .
Amen—He called twice, for third time he pronounced my full name "Amen Iraqi Hosseini?" with a tone of small question mark this time.
It was a relief to hear my full name at this distant land—Amen Iraqi Hosseini

Wow!

I reacted to him. I didn't know that the guy whom we had avoided all our time at the mills playground could have been found here at this Ajit Juneja's academy.
Did he had that spinning quality?

Ayan—I sighed with the quality of moment.
He gave me a space of silence allowing me to continue and ponder on seeing this old chap.
He was looking handsome, a perfect independent.
"Let's go for a coffee," he invited, and it was enough to ascribe this person. He had that little hint of American accent. Going for a coffee is always an above average people's fashion.

Practice was over and we went for a coffee.

From Biratnagar, he had moved to Delhi through study sponsors. He worked in a call centre and played cricket.

There was no much of history as yet in his life, it was plain and simple unlikely mine.

I realized how good was that delivery when he had bowled me 6 years back in the mills playground. He was suddenly changing the whole impression that I had towards him.

Life was beautiful. I did realize seeing this man.

He was vying for the same goal as a spinner, in the Indian national side.

What a companion I had got. A young boy who was not acting any fake, carrying a true determination, wholesome independent, perfectly courageous, not addicted to useless facebook and orkut.

Things happen quick in big cities.

I got shifted with him in his rented home—Ayan, Amen and Majid.

This third guy was Ayan's friend.

Majid was Ayan's call centre-mate as well.

The shifting was nothing alike my childhood time that I had seen; no heavy materials to carry rather everything that I owned was enough to be packed in a plastic bag.

For livelihood, I joined the same call centre where Ayan and Majid worked.

These call centre's are surely best thing in the world. One needed no degree, vacant seats almost always available and you groom perfect with speaking skills in your first job.

The salary was around 10000/—enough to put my mind in the state of *'mungerilal ke haseen sapne'*

We talked to Americans on phone acting as we were calling from Florida. In trainings, we were made to believe that U.S people were the dumbest of all, they sometimes thrashed us with slang words which to the first-timers may have sounded as a privilege to have been hearing from a foreigner. Our accent had to be sounding like a U.S localite; but as soon as we saw an Indian surnamed guy like Patel, we didn't keep ourselves away from cashing in—"Are you from India, sir?"

But this magic of bhai-bhai never worked here in this professional field; Majid who on my first day was 3 cubicles away engineered with a smart smile, "go and complain to Sunny Deol—a person isn't cooperating in the notion of being an Indian"

This was business.

Two months of time had gone. The time wasn't bad. I had sent 3 letters at home about my well being. practice at Juneja's academy was good. If I was discouraged at my first sight then with passing time and crucified training I was growing well above them. The pace with which I started bowling was not at all easy to play for batsmen who even played those shots all day and night.

As the practice session would start, I was given the prestige of bowling with the new bowl.

I was suddenly the talked about person.

I smarted and patronized infront of boys.

This was the story of just one academy, there were hundreds of them and in that thousands of talent.

If you see a dream, you are a dreamer. If you believe in your dreams, you are hopeful. If you pursue your dreams, you are courageous. I had reached to this courageous point, going further and describing further needed lots of heart.

The best times were back again. In the gym, practice, call centre everywhere things were good and fine. And most of all, namaz was leading to satisfaction.

Of my lived life, one thing I have learned finely is that whatever happens in our lives-good or bad whatever; if we are not at peace and satisfied then there is something wrong going on.

In our schooling days, principal personally updated "quote of the week" very much like today we update our facebook status.

From many, one line that still triggers today is—"Before you actually win, it is necessary that you smell victory"

Now how do we smell victory??

To have been smelling victory is not an easy task at all.

The local tournaments were registering good performances of mine; enough to leave a mark on people's mind.

I had spent very small time here and I did know that even one year of time wasn't fulfilling to what I was trying for.

Furthermore, I wouldn't have only been trying for the Indian national side but also in one of the toughest competing sectors in the world.

Things were tough and so it was worth trying.

By this time call centre job was getting exhausted on mind. Everyday going into the same ridicule cubicle and talking to dumb people was getting on my nerves. Every minute the fake of being an American localite was disturbing. The alter time table of sleeping in the afternoons was scoffy.

I couldn't have left the job just like that either as it was giving me the vital surviving money but I couldn't have clutched on to this job forever.

For some days of time, I decided to dedicate my 2 hours of time in the afternoon to find any newspaper, magazine or anything alike for where they can hire me to write articles. I had a little background of writing back in Nepal having written 14 articles for a national daily there.

If I got any sort of this job here, it would have been less time consuming and lots of space for my brain to work in an inventive field.

Couple of days I noted the names of newspaper and magazines, did my homework for where I could try with the addresses and detail.

I noted down addresses of different offices, though I was unfamiliar to which place they were and when I would know where places were, 2 hours of allotted time looked very less to travel.

Delhi was a big place afterall.

"Always start with best in the business," I invented this formula.

But I couldn't implement.

When I reached Gurgaon finding the building of 'The times of India' I felt as the most idiot person standing there when everybody was so much busy in the humdrums of news making.

I felt big idiot when I thought reality. There was no vacancy at this moment in this office, I didn't have any degree, no writing courses done, no worldly or aged experiences with life, achiever of nothing; yet I was standing here thinking of a job and all upon what—In Times of India.

My God!

On first day, I was tranquilizing into poor thoughts.

No successful person has ever given up on his first attempt and no failed person has ever mounted back again from the first blocks of failure.

That's the only and little difference.

It is about 'keep on trying'

Next morning at 6, after having done with namaz and before readying to sleep after the call centre session—I opened Majid's laptop, youtube.com, typed—"Motivational videos"

List of videos fluttered and I chose "If you have never failed, you have never lived"

I don't know how does this happen, how does this mind at once changes the whole perception and how do we feel so comfortable in failing. I don't know!

I felt heated up back again.

I slept at peace after that, feeling secured and bounty.

By 12, I woke up and by 12.20 out for the catch again with the notified places in a piece of paper that I may have made to reach in this little 2 hours of time.

Bus, tempo gave a pride about struggling. So many people, some happy, some sad, some giggling, some intense, some thinking, some thoughtless, some pale, some blackened. All shades of life present and there in between—'YOU' thinking "Which genre of person do I belong to?"

Whatever the genre of mine have been, I was still trying, I was still on the run.

Lot of here and there efforts went for days.

I made a proposal in which it was briefed that I wanted to write in youth motivating matters. I had two of that kind; one for the newspaper in which I had proposed to write weekly in a specified column and the other proposal was for a magazine in which I had proposed to write monthly.

Honestly, these proposals were nothing. It was just a license to be able to meet the editor and rest of the things depended upon impressing that person with the confidence of doing something.

The proposal was too much ambitious, technically no newspaper or magazine could have given me a chance to write when already they had employed more learned people than me. I knew that.

I was too over ambitious but my point was to get in a meeting with them and I could sway them in my talk; that was the confidence with which I was moving.

That confidence paid up nowhere; sometimes suggesting it is your stupidity when people laughed upon my proposal. Sometimes look from people would be 'I admire that you have dared to reach here with this proposal but at the end of the day, you're stupid'

I just clinged on to the confidence waiting for the right man to meet up. It happened, it happened when I met the editor of 'Delhi beats' magazine.

I conspired to him, "I am young and I want to write with the same perspective.

As a youth, I don't want a worldly experienced guy who have had his experiences with the world at some point of time to stand up and tell 'this is how you should do it'

I prefer—the same era guy, no superman, nobody special rather just one of us to stand up and tell this is how I am doing it"

Among all the editors I met so far, he was the best listener. He patiently replied to me with a little stretch of smile on his face, "I do believe in mad dreamer's achievement"

That was it!
Here I got the response positive, I was waiting for this man.
He talked much more and finally gave me a chance to write an article and if that gets selected, I shall be legible to join 'Delhi Beats'
This magazine was published twice in a month. Salary was good. Routine work wasn't necessary.
Articles that I showed up which I had written in Nepali national daily were impressive and turned out very handy.

I went home and told my room mates about it. They were proud and I was worried.
Stakes were high and in that one article, everything depended.
Just when I was getting nothing on mind; I took Majid's laptop, opened youtube and listened to Imran khan speeches, then turned into some of India today's page and things like this.
"Not to copy-paste any material but to encourage myself and have that writing mind into operations," I answered Majid not to give him wrong impressions.

When pen was guided into paper structuring words and when words in paper travelled through editor's eye, he thought something I don't know what and readied to take me in.
"I've done it," that is what I spelt in the message box texting to Ayan and Majid from my cell phone.

Delhi beats was my new home.
I had to write only 2 articles a month, stories and ideas to be given by the editor.
So, I had done it.

The small done things are a loud echo for a wayfarer.
Now again the pleasures of routine had changed.
When 10 O'clock at night, Majid and Ayan started getting ready for their call centre session in proper boots and formal attire to talk with Americans; that time I readied with my nightsuit for a tight-right time sleep.
They looked at me with bizzare, nothing with jealous eyes but only with eyes conveying 'you are lucky'

We might have separated our ways at night as sleeping and working individuals but I and Ayan always got up together at 3 in the afternoon in Juneja's academy at Kashmiri gate ground.
Whereas, Majid's time to talk just started with his probable girlfriend—Richa, a call centre mate from rich family working only as a hobby.
Majid and Richa were the best people to campaign for fevicol, they were stuck and it was hard to see a phone-less moment.
I don't know how they talked so much and what they talked about. Majid would give a missed call and Richa instantly called back. She had newly come out from the shells of teenage tantrums, excited to have been a grown-up, new into seemingly love-flirt stuffs. Both felt so cool to have been talking to each other. Majid's laugh never contracted all the while he talked on the phone. It was their favorite past-time, hobby, passion and so it was everything for them. It was their busy-ness of the mind.

Whereas, I and Ayan would be serious here at Juneja's academy. Our busy-ness was different. Ayan was growing into a good spinner with lot of loop and flight in the air tending batsmen to have a go at one point or other in the match. I respected his skills with the bowl, he supported me as well.

The philosophy 'of you rise from where you fail' was planted on my mind due to this man.

In a match where he was bowling usual as to what he used to bowl, he was hit 4 sixes in five balls by a tail-ender; even though he was bowling to a perfect line, all the five balls were exactly same. I went up to him and said, "Ayan, you need to change something with the delivery being bowled"

He was yet composed and inscripted to this line in his own head—"You rise from where you fail"

He took the wicket at the last bowl.

He had to hear lot of things for how he had bowled in that over, but if you have ever been a student; I am not talking about student of some scrappy school or a scrumptuous college where scoring marks and getting a degree is how you receive the education.

I am talking about a student, if you have ever been to yourself, having that zeal to learn and yearn to perspire, if you have ever been then there was a lesson to be learnt—"You rise from where you fail"

We never came in the lines of competition for one another. He was an orthodox spinner and I was a genuine medium fast bowler.

After practices, we went for fruit drinks and other healthy food stuffs. Often we dined outside.

We had a lovely life.

Only thing that I missed on all this while was a girl(friend). I didn't feel loneliness at any time but yes, I felt girl-loneliness.

Now this is a different form of loneliness. Apart from studs, toughness and roughness—sensitiveness, grace and beauty is a different thing to miss.

Things would stark more strongly when I saw these growing love buds—Majid and Richa talking.

I would think about Nikita, my beautiful class mate at one time.

Then some more girls ran onto the same thought but Nikita had always been the prime of all.

In Delhi, girls were good as well. I liked intellectual girls, those who were real strong.

But pity that I never did find them in call centre arena, nor obviously did I find them in the cricket games.

They were best to be found at colleges or in big offices.

Girls that I would mostly see were not intellectuals at all, they were frozen in the fashion world of less clothing strolled in the culture of lotsa crushes before you have a boyfriend and then lotsa boyfriend before you get a hubby.

The kind of wonderful girls am talking about are usual to be seen in journalism field and the reason I specifically say 'journalism' is because now I work in 'Delhi beats' and the reason am so much preaching about intellectuality is because I have just seen Mallika today.

My god!

"Mallika"—Let me try and define you in my way.
She had all rights from the 'love legislation book' to have her name kept as Mallika.

Paulo Coelho's definition of Jezebel in his book was little less infront of her in terms of beauty.

I had taken more time to be Rahul Dravid's fan in my childhood than to be her fan in adulthood.

Flower rose wasn't the epitomy and prosed example of beauty because this girl belonged to the same earth.

Mallika was on earth. I was unable to imagine a girl that we will meet in heavens as our gifts as promised by God, who will happen to be one thousand times gracious and beautiful than any girl on earth.

I am surely overspoken but I don't mind anything for the moment.

I am 10 day new to Delhi Beats, a new intern walks in with a covering on her head, a piece of scarf that is called as hijab, sharing her new ideas in the general meeting about the cover story with subel sharma.

I was dazzlingly impressed.

The little breakage of sentences while she spoke was so lovely to ears, the frame of sight on which eyes saw this girl was a lucky frame of shot to eyes, the mixture of sensitiveness and boldness was the best mix God could have fusioned.

I could imagine all my life in a stage if I can have this girl.

Damn to the one year of time to return home, damn Nikita, damn everything in world, damn to my Indian cricket determination.

The intoxication wasn't there just in the alcohol.

I told Ayan about this fantastic girl, he was sad because he was alone in the race now. I and Majid both had girls on mind but still he was girl-less.

Damn to his loneliness, damn emotions!!

I was largely toxicated on seeing her.

Practice wasn't having my attention and article writing didn't look as my domain of craftiness.

Girls surely are amazing, they have the power.

I needed to come into senses. I did come.

God's stipulation of that 5 times a day of namaz is incredible. It is just at times when people may think 'how disturbing it is' but it is simply incredible and that's really the testing for If my creation gets so much enjoined in the happiness or sadness or whatever emotions of human nature that he forgets me—God? Does his busy-ness of the world changes?

Now what namaz does is; it gives us back our refreshing time.

God is GOD and he must not have been unmindful to give us this five minute activity in between our work and sleep.

I did come out of the one hour crazy intoxication of Mallika after Asr namaz although she was on my mind constant

With all these activities, three months of time had gone. Days were passing fast and quick alike everything in this city.

My first article was published. I took the half page of a magazine titled as 'Ambition matters in life'

I had written and captured a 'wow' effect through that.

It was an achievement.

Mallika had not given any reactions personally as she did not know me at all nor she did know that there was a volcano eruption going on my mind for her, she was completely unaware even of my existence.

Life was going good.
'Three months of time had gone' I had to pierce this notion to myself.
"3 months!"
Three emotional letters was sent at home. I had almost found that perfect girl. I had settled with my earnings well and fine. Everything was on order.

By this time, Richa had come closer to Majid. They had started meeting more often. Majid on his laptop now had Richa's photo in the display screen background.
I had seen Richa in the call centre arena when I used to work there but this photo that she had sent was hilarious. The photo had gone from a strict selection process conditioning to hippy and cool quotients, a typical cornered eye pose with victory sign that I don't know why girls put in their every shot, little red dimple cheeks with a natural rosiness as it looked—thanks to the good beauty parlors of Delhi, all attempts from that one photo to show 'You are lucky to have me'
But the prized thing in that photo was not Richa at all, it was her dog who stood beside in the picture and which was the reason of calling this photo 'hilarious' His name as I could read in the caption was 'Richa and Taggy'
That dog was a piece of art. Hair straightening machine was first tested on his tail, colour check to attain perfect green while she started painting was first checked in the inside belly portion of taggy, his ears and legs had extra fur put on by Miss Richa complying to the effect of dog's status. I had better named this dog 'experimental'

They had bought his jolly looking face through pedigrees and the provided privileges of dog home.

Away from dog's story, there were much more interesting aspects to my story; this thing was told to me by Ayan very rightly.

He once shuffled in the question, "Do you have any idea what is going in your home?"

I had hints but I did not want to know exactly from that angle of thought.

I only said to him, "It was one of the most satisfying moments of time travelling history when I left home and I can believe in my satisfaction.

Maybe after one year when I go home, I will have surprised changes awaiting.

Maybe!"

Next two months was hectic. Lot of club and other tournaments was scheduled. Some in Jharkhand, Bihar, Kerela and many other states in different tournaments. We had won the ones in Bihar and of Jharkhand but had lost in Kerela.

All the while in tours, I had caught up with my work. It was then that I came in contact with Mallika through adding a cc of my article emails to her address. Through this, she came to know that I am a cricketer of a good level, a working individual and in a way came to know me. I was far in places playing cricket. A very good experiece being badged up. We were a great team. I was the charmed opener bowler with the new ball.

Back to Delhi after cricketing tours was less soothing. After months of travelling, coming back home didn't make me feel in anyway that I was back at home. There was no motherly treatment awaiting, there was no father to ask the pinpoint details, there was no brother to mark the feeling or signify the presence of a trustworthy companion nearby.

I started with my regular office work again being present physically and not only through emails. Five months had gone in total.

7 more months was left before I could have reached to the deadline of one year in lieu of presenting a form of life to everybody.

We don't know what life gives us—A slap, thunderbolt or a chilling winter breeze.
Whatever was on the offer, I was taking and grabbing it instantly.

I had never been forgetful for what my responsibilities should be towards my home. I always had this thing in mind about the hefty loans that was upon dad and which was the top most priority of any of my brothers including me.
We don't exactly know upon what we conspire our dreams or demands. It is subconscious.

As a youth, I was afflicted to get in the biggest stage of all: Indian Cricket team
If any of us gave up in the mid way, would it mean that we gave up?
Maybe it would mean!!

If any of us strictly realized that it was only about 11 out of millions and then we gave up . . . would it still mean, we gave up?

Maybe!!

If any of us decides not to languish in that strict requirement, would it yet mean we gave up?

Maybe it would still mean . . .

I was started to this argument when 3 successive losses were faced in one of the tournaments where stakes were very high. I was actually doubting if I could have made it. There looked lot better cricketers than me.

Upon that, 1 year of sweltering time looked meager though I could have acquired more time if I had the chance but I would have no remarkable thing to show dad that this is what I have done in this 1 year of leased time that I had taken.

I needed something substantial.

Working in 'Delhi Beats' was fine but it wasn't an achievement proportionate to my home leaving event.

I had raised the bars of competition a little too high when nobody was expecting anything from me. Never had father nor anyone asked me to do such and such great things but in my own high bars, I was getting caged.

Things were fearful. I was fairly afraid if I might get trapped in between all of this. The most fantastic girl that I had been admiring may never be with me. The commitments, promises, determination that I had shown by leaving home could all add to the laughing stock. My collection in the events of failureness could have added one more chapter if I left this dream hereon.

Oh my God!

Where is the simple life that people live? I want to live that . . .

"Millions try for their place in the national team, not everybody get their place"

This was it when my business mind came into operations.

I thought to set up something of my own to be secured with further events of life.

I wasn't feeling exhausted with my work at Delhi beats or even if I was, it must have been for good.

The idea of doing something is not an idea at all, it's only the first step.

I thought about many business ideas. When I travelled in bus, I would see things around, the pinpointed details. From naught bolts to giant buses—from chai-wala stalls to sky-scraping buildings.

There were many things that constituted in the making of a building or a giant bus. Anything could be picked and business was started.

But things were not easy and it dared not be easy as well.

So, I learned one thing very apprehensively: Before capturing the most perfect idea, you gotta have hundred flop ideas.

And soon, I had so many flop ideas; from exporting coconuts to coconut shells, making burgers to manufacturing shoes. I had all sorts of flop ideas coming and going.

I had to keep in mind that I had no money as well; only thing I had was willingness to develop an idea. That's it.

After more than two week of this idea disease that had propelled in my mind, I got the perfect one.

I took Majid's laptop and typed UNIQUE EMBASSY

Yes, this was the idea, the perfect one.

Unique Embassy—its aim was to open a big store in a very prime location in which each country's most defining product would be showcased and available for sale in subsidised prices. Like Khukuri, Nepali cultural dress, Nepali paper(Lokta) diaries for Nepal, such way every country's most representable item, an item that distinguished and marked an identification of each country. Financially run by concerned embassies.

I had started working on this project; I started taking the appointment dates from concerned embassies. It was a good potential idea.

The project was okay, not being wholly sounding like a professional project but again an ambitious one. Again, I was dependent upon my convincing power. Convincing was the whole game.

You can sell ice in the himalayas only if you could convince that ice unlike water can take shapes and so someone forwarded themselves to make igloos in the himalayas.

Now, here were many things that I was taking care of. Firstly my cricket, then my job, then my new business proposal, then Mallika.

Ayan had asked me to rate it according to priorities.

I couldn't do that. I didn't know which to prioritize and which to sideline comparatively.

Cricket was something that I had left home for initially, Delhi beats job was my surviving money, Business proposal could just have been my form of life to take to dad, Mallika was that perfect girl with whom I had seen my life in a stage. Everything needed the same amount of focus.

Mallika was adherant to namaz even in office which was pretty impressive. I would whole day in office gaze at her, she was addictive.

When the clock gonged near to five, peon dropping off the lights of some cabin, some people straightening their back, women suddenly realizing the need to re-make-up 'as it's now time to go in the open air infront of men,' sun at the window in its cherry color done with the 9 to 5 job of providing light too announcing—"I'm off"

Just then, I would realize that it is now time to go, time to go away, time to go away from office and most importantly time to go away from Mallika.

It was hard to see her going away.

What if I might not turn up tomorrow, what if she is gone by tomorrow, what if some calamity strucks and we both are unable to witness the other day, what if something something happens and this becomes my last chance of having seen her. What if!

I had thought this filmy way many a times but never had those calamities struck. I would everyday ridiculously stand there at 5, watch her and think the same thing exactly with the same delusion of thought.

The only near to love-shayari by mom would hit me at this time in a humming slow melody at the background.

Aap ko jaate na dekha jaayega
Shamma ko pehle bujhate jaiye..

We talked not so often because she wasn't the next door girl. She was reserved and had certain sanctity intact to her character. I loved that. I loved every bit of her unavailability.

On 1st march, I met Nasrina Khatoon of Bangladesh embassy. This was my first meeting about the project. I chose Bangladesh embassy very carefully as my first discussion ground to correctly weigh the seriousness that an embassy would take upon the project.

She was the 1st secretary of the embassy and she was more excited than me regarding the project. It looked involving for them when I said—This is every embassy's chance to come and interact with the public directly showcasing their respective country's diverse nature.

She even made me know about the *khadi* clothe that Mahatma Gandhi used to wear belonging from the then undivided part of India-Bangladesh, which was quite historical to know.

My first meeting was damn successful. They were ready to incur the funds that according to my project, all embassies had to pay.

I remarked dad's vital experience in words, "Make a move" Some embassies even had separate funds for inventional projects as these. Majid's laptop was marking its advantage helping me to find from embassies' address to each country's identifying and defining products.

With more meetings, the talk was getting betterly versed, the project was getting more professional and the belief was getting more deterrent.

After 1 month, I was near to perfect professional. D.L Associates had done fabulous paper work including the contracts. Seven embassies had come into my badge having signed the pre-confirmation contract.

I needed 12 to complete my project. It wasn't hard; I got them on hand within 3 weeks.

So, everything was finalized. I asked Ayan to leave his call centre job and help me in administering the project, he was more than happy to align into the right time working schedule.

On 18th April evening, I and Ayan sat down at our home with the copies of pre confirmed contracts on our hands.

Oh my God!!

Those piece of papers had thousand morale stories to tell. To have been reaching to such an agreement was awesome. Our 12 embassies were ready. 5 lakh per embassy. List of significant products were decided. Products to be coordinated and brought upon by respective embassies from their countries.

Now, we had to bring the leased papers of allotted location, the actual agreement and rest all the formalities.

I had deadlined the opening of this store on 1st of july, goods and products to be delivered by respective embassies before 1st of june, half amount cheques to be given by the same date—1st of june and collection of post dated cheques of not later than 15th of july. These were deadlines that were set.

I had to be thoroughly sounding like professional and a hardliner. Not giving too much of flexibilities where it wasn't needed.

Ayan was assigned these tidbits of jobs, he was helping me to keep affairs in order.

Things alike everything in city was happening fast and quick. The pace was too fast even to think how exactly was I doing such big things. I had stopped going to the cricket practices on all this while. I was focused to deliver this one important thing.

Majid was still happy to be doomed with his call centre job in the lavishness of rich Richa.

For my project, the place was finalized, it was a big mall where our store was to charm up. Interior designer Sweta Rao had already started with her bright ideas of placing stuffs where and how.

She had exactly understood what I wanted out of this store. Rich people should look at the goods and products here as something subtly artistic, mediocre and students should look here as 'stuffs available are distinctive' and others should fantasize to have been shopping here marking a privilege.

She was exactly working with this idea.

A lame should never think 'how to walk' instead what should I do when I walk.

A blind should never thinks 'how to see' instead 'what should I see when I see.

God always gives those chances. Either this way or that way.

We gotta keep our hopeful quotients well alive.

All this while, I was rattling into one dilemma.

Should I stop aspiring to get in the Indian cricket team now?

Would it mean that I failed, if I do that?

Any problem's staunchest feature is that it looks as if that's the biggest problem. And really it is sometimes.

I have always been an opposition to the notion of 'soldiers are meant to die in wars for their country'

Why . . .

Is death the point of success?

I had to be mindfully passionate and not unmindfully patriotic.

My relations with Abraar Khan, CEO of D.L. Associates was growing very good. He had every faith on me regarding Unique Embassy, he was thoroughly convinced about the vision of the project.

He was masticated with the idea of Unique embassy as an enterprise and a potential project that could be developed all over the world as a franchisee.

I had partnered with him in the project. This was very needful as I was alone here with no reputation of business background infront of anybody. I needed somebody's hand for people to believe on me or else no embassies would have finalized the whole agreement upon that a boy named Amen has a great idea and so let's give him money for the project.

No, it couldn't have ever happened that way.

He was same as to my father's age built strongly in physique. He was sheerly driven by my enthusiasm and I was appalled by his honesty.

He had every chance of running the project alone at any point after getting the idea and any embassy would have supported him anyway because he was an established person, having a name and reputation of their enterprise since 20 years.

God really conspires us to reach where we are destined to reach.

The boy who failed in 9th class having finished his schooling with all sorts of dissatisfaction, the boy who is a drop-out from college, the boy who left home for an unprecedented dream, that boy is establishing an enterprise and that too not of a small sort but with a vision that has potential to create franchisees all over the world.

God should be appalled by the story but then he happens to be the director of every man's film.

All this while though I had left going for cricket practices, but I had caught up with my writing job at Delhi Beats.

Even if I had no time, then also I would somehow manage and write articles on the given topics, it was really something I loved.

I would fight and quarrel with my editor over the ideas and viewpoints that exactly needed to be delivered to the youths.

He loved that as well. It would grill our minds and show us different paths that could be discovered.

I had got a very fine appreciation by my editor, subel sharma—"If all the youths of Delhi were at the right direction, you would have been in their nerves"

I would mostly fight against the wrong fashion in everything that was getting developed, the sayably modernity and not implicative modernity that was at rise, the total exclusion of experience i.e. old age in comparison to the youths.

These days generation craved for change unrealizing that sometimes change is not needed at all.

They were just strolling in the new world order to mark their presence felt but just that they never knew what exactly to do.

"We start up with something and we end up doing something else" was the most highlighted statement that I made in my father's advise turned into an article—"Make a move"

Mallika had beautiful eyes. I never would forget them. Those were my motivation point.

All the work was going with full heart and soul, nobody was lazy into it, nobody was engrossed into useless stuffs, everybody realizing the importance of delivering this one important project of their lives, everybody were focused.

A UNIQUE EMBASSY was getting formed.

I wanted to share this with my dad or other members of the family but I was inaccessible in all terms.

Mallika with colorful hijab on her head and the glow of not so white but gracious face gulping between the hijab and shoulder said to me—"You write really fantastic articles. I really admire you"

This was first interjection of compliments from her face to face. It was very late but no problems.

I had to carefully not think too much about her because I needed to have focus on this one important project of my life.

My contact and network was growing hi-fi. I was slowly switching into another dream.

With all sorts of ongoing activities came 1st of June, the time when belief was accredited into bank account.
The half payment came; alongwith the delivery of products that were mutually enlisted to be delivered by the same date.
Wow!!

All beliefs on me was getting justified.
When I had left home, One year was ofcourse a very small time but if you have that determination, even little time looks plenty enough.

I had left home for something else, but I was getting into something else.
Many times we dream something and live something else.
After making a move, God just affixes us on the perfect spot.
As a passionate child, we are raw dreamers.
Fraction percentage, exactly get their childhood dream and most people flip their dream to make a perfect one.
It's about making a move.
In this decade, we are hypnotized by magnificient sounding words like dream and success not realizing what actually they are.
Where do we stop dreaming?
Or at what point do we really consider ourselves failure?

Abraar Khan was full time involved in this project. Sweta Rao was done with her fabulous emphatic work. We had to be in consistent touch with the embassies, keep entertaining them and assure different embassies about the equal weightage being given to all 12 embassies in the store.

The products were from rare fishes to glitzy khukuris. Each product looked romantic in their spots at the stored warehouse. Each item looked as if they were all waiting with eager to get into the showcases of Unique Embassy. They all rejoicing and thanking to the idea that has come up by me having now potentiality to actually subserve the whole world.

I realized, "you fail for a purpose"

At one time of life, I was dismayed at time's feature of passing everything quickly but today I was jubilant as it was nearing me to 1st of July.

The date when my hard work comes into open air.

Everything was set just that time hadn't come as yet.

It came, alike all things, this time came up as well.

On 1st of July, UNIQUE EMBASSY was formed.

Everything was right about it. The products staged under showcase boxes crawled a thanks giving speech to me, officials of embassies were proud of their 'Yes' that they had nodded when I had approached and made them understand the project, 50 year old Abraar Khan's decision of attaching his services to a 20—year Amen was justified.

My mom from her shayari book had read out at one time-

Kehne ko zindagi thi bahut mukhtasar magar
Kuch yoon basar hui ki khuda yaad aagaya..

At that time, I had always thought about one side of this story that the time in life was less and it was hard, but to this day I was realizing that time is always plenty and life is not so hard.

For sure, the nature of God has come knowing to me.

It was a superhit proven idea. All magazines, newspapers jammed in with the success story of this idea.

On 15th of July, other half payment was received. By 3rd august, a franchisee call was received from a private investor from France.

Things were in order more than I had assumed.

There was still time left before my one year of stipulated time to return home would have completed.

I couldn't contain myself anymore.

I e-mailed the last one at home—*"I am returning home"*

One month before the stipulated time, I reached home. There is no joy better, there is no accomplishment bigger, there is no feat higher to see parent's proud faces yet again.

I was at home. There were questions in abundance and I had answers to all of them.

Last chapter

$\mathcal{B}$ack to this chilly winter morning of 26 december, 2011; shaking me out of reverential reverie was my wife—Mallika.

"Come in for breakfast," punched a sweet and sharp voice.

I saw all around me, it was still foggy. The sun was still bright.

I queried to myself with disbelief, "What was it that made God to hand over me this secret—I am now a member of heavens"
I am now a member of heavens..!!?

This was my life. I as yet don't know at what point did almighty decide to give me this honor, this jubilation.
Or maybe there is no particular point in life where you get your life into heavens or hell, there is no point where you fail or succeed, there is only one journey that you keep defining by living.

I was now assured to see the real achievement quotient from life in the hell's face for what I have missed before going inside the heavens.

Words and teaching of mom would see its reality.

Now, I will await the judgment day and all those days in silence. I can't imagine the day when this secret will get realized. All emotions will surely fail to describe and all assumptions will fail to picturize for what I may achieve.

For sure, God directs the movie!! The movie of a Raw Dreamer . . .